JOY RE-AWAKENED

Books by Rosalie Deer Heart

Healing Grief ~A Mother's Story

Harvesting Your Journals with Alison Strickland

Awaken Your All Knowing Heart

Soul Befriending

Living Future Pull

Celebrating The Soul of CPSI with Doris Shallcross

Affective Education Guidebook with Bob Eberle

Affective Direction with Bob Eberle

**To order your autographed copies, visit my website at
www.heart-soul-healing.com**

Praise for *Joy Re-Awakened*

"Pack your bags with an open heart, curiosity, and gratitude for the pilgrimage that is *Joy Re-Awakened*. Rosalie Deer Heart invites us to recognize that the magic ingredient to discovering and living into our deepest states of Grace and Joy is to learn to edge-walk through our lives. Rosie's openness, candor, and sharing of her own pilgrimage home to Joy is an invitation to us to explore our own edges and walk them. Doing so is the greatest gift we can give to ourselves and each other, and thankfully our guide has shown us how. En-Joy!"

—**Lou Ann Daly,** author of *Humans Being*

Rosalie Deer Heart's newest book, *Joy Re-Awakened,* spans the experiences and wisdom of more than seven decades of Personal, Edge-Walking, and Blissful Soul Stories. Her candor as she revisits Journal Entries from her past is refreshing, thought-provoking and inspirational. In this book she quotes Sam Keen in *Fire in the Belly*, saying, "Nothing shakes our journeys through life so much as the questions we ask." Thank you, Rosie, for challenging us with just the right questions to help us evolve into our individual and collective Soul Stories.

—**Diane Jackman Skolfield,** author of *Nine Months Ago Was Yesterday,* and Intuitive Wellness Counselor

Rosalie Deer Heart has been a professional colleague, friend and sister seeker for four decades. As such, I have had the great privilege of not only reading all of her (now eleven) books detailing her amazing spiritual unfolding over time, but also of watching from a front row seat and often following in her tracks. Hers is a powerful story of how Spirit collaborates with us in becoming our most authentic, courageous, and joyful selves. In *Joy Re-Awakened,* she meticulously walks her readers through the process of how she has "broken rank" with ancestral family patterns and beliefs and cultural norms to create a life that is deeply and truly spirit-centered, full of grace, and enspirited by joy. She inspires me to do the same, and I trust she will do that for all readers of a book so relevant to our times.

—**Meredith Jordan,** Creator of The Living Spiritual Elders Project

Joy Re-Awakened has helped me understand things about myself, my own journey, and purpose in this lifetime. It takes concepts from higher levels of consciousness and brings them down to our third dimensional expression so that we can understand them, work with them, and apply them in our lives.

—**Dr. Gladys McGarey,** Founder of The Foundation
for Living Medicine

With honesty, courage, and heart, Rosalie Deer Heart has marked the trail for those of us who want to break rank with the limitations of the past and begin the journey back to a state of joy. *Joy Re-Awakened* is a compelling tale of one woman's lived truth as she walks the zig-zagging path toward happiness, a story that includes amazing super-natural adventures, challenging internal struggles, and the constant, loving support of unseen spirit guides. This book is a practical guide for seekers everywhere trying to understand how to push through the boundaries of their personal stories and move into the spaciousness of the authentic self—the soul story. Read it not only for the fascinating anecdotes but also its insights on how to find joy in whatever life presents and experience its most transcendent moments.

—**M. K. Welsch,** author of *Sacred Journey*

During a pandemic, a book about JOY is sorely needed. Fear contracts us and can prevent us from being open to expansive joy. A world that suddenly turned unpredictable and scary, facing tragedy and loss needs balance. Rosie gives us a plan and tools to find these places within ourselves. One key is the connection of Joy and the Sacred. As our world transforms into a new version of itself, what better guidebook than *Joy Re-Awakened* to steer our way.

—**Arla Patch,** author of *A Body Story*

Joy
Re-Awakened

ROSALIE DEER HEART

HEART LINK
PUBLICATIONS

ABOUT THE COVER ART

"The painting represents our spiritual pathways through life. On the top left hand side of the painting is a Heart and an Angel representing the chakras of love and healing. DNA symbols are on the right side. The bottom of the painting is the garden where we plant our seeds. Seven crystals and crystal seeds on the bottom of the painting represent the seven chakras.

The crystal seed with the Rainbow are the colors within us. The bigger crystal on the right with the mountain inside the crystal seed represents the mountain we climb in life. The middle is the fire spirit of the sun."

—**Colin Hall**
www.colinhallart.com

To

Susan Ortiz for your love of life,
generosity, and exuberance for dance.

Deb Stanley for your courage, full faith, and joy.

You each continue to be Way Showers to me.

To members of Glad Helpers—past, present, and future—
who serve as channels of blessings as we offer daily, healing prayers
to people and countries world wide.

Contents

CHAPTER THREE: Soul Story

Foreword

The 2020 COVID-19 pandemic invaded the world as I began editing this book. I am an empath and I grieved as people died. Fear and uncertainty captured the headlines and challenged our ways of experiencing and expressing our connections. Gathering and celebrating family and community became dangerous overnight.

I experience this time as both a heart breaking time and a heart opening time. When I allowed myself to feel the pain, suffering, and uncertainty, I realized that compassion fatigue was real. When I remembered to be aware of gratitude, I learned that Edge-Walking between the dark and the light was a way to move beyond fear to embrace love, faith, and Joy.

"What is mine to do?" echoed in my waking life and my dreamtime. *Joy Re-Awakened* was my answer.

In order to dare to publish this book, I had to override the cantankerous voice in my head that screamed, "How arrogant and crazy to publish a book about Joy when millions of people are experiencing the opposite."

When I breathed my way through that light dimming inner voice, another familiar voice arose and challenged, "Who do you think you are?"

I am a namer, a dream mapper, and when I am in alignment with my soul, I am a cosmic catalyst. I am also a lover of Truth and I believe that Joy is one of Love's gifts.

I offer this story of my journey as a way to uplift consciousness and embrace the future as a place of revelation—not fear.

Deep Bows of Appreciation To

Sandra Clark for your keen attention to details, your patience, and your ability to call me to task when needed.

Diane Jackman, Alison Strickland, Diane Powell, Alison Ray, and Jean McKillop for your valuable suggestions and support.

Colin Hall for your creative vision and service.

Janice St. Marie and Joe Mowrey for your creative talents and generosity.

Introduction

The world needs more Joy. I believe we were all born Precious and over time many of us conformed to mediocrity and our small Personal Story. I believe there is more to life than being alive. I also believe that we are each individual strands in the web of life.

I remember being born to be a channel of Joy. Then I forgot. Take heart, because once I graduated from the trance of limiting Personal Story, I reclaimed being a magnet for Joy and followed Emily Dickinson, a poet, who wrote, "Find ecstasy in life."

For me, Joy is a state of Being. I also experience Joy as the outer expression of inner love that manifests as radiance.

I am curious about how the remembrance of radiance and Joy might transform and heal our fragmented Selves and the world. As an apprentice of Joy, I challenge myself with the question, "What is the Joy potential?" before I make a choice.

I am convinced that we were each born with a Joy gene. Along my journey, Joy became an acquaintance and, over time, a familiar. Furthermore, I believe that an essential part of our unique soul agreement is to embody our unique Joy strand of expression for the evolution of our individual souls as well as the evolution of our planet. Drumroll for Mirabai Starr, author of *Wild Mercy*, who reminded me about the connection between boldness and Joy, writing: "Embolden our heart so we can be in the world in the most joyful way."

Sustaining a Joy perspective in our uncertain and divided world feels revolutionary. Honoring my connection to my Joy gene in a culture that demands instant answers and ninety second sound bites was hard work. With lots of inner work and outer action, I gradually claimed and reclaimed a Joy perspective. The question that kept circling me was: "How do I align with my Soul Story and cleave to it when I am aware that I am leaking energy?"

As a dutiful daughter, I shut down my Joy for conditional love. As a friend, I reined in my Joy because I didn't want to risk jealousy. As a lover, I held back my Joy because I did not want to risk overwhelming my partner. Later as a wife, I traded my Joy for stability and more conditional love. As a mother, I encouraged and applauded Joy in my children and wrote about my own Joy sightings in my journal. As a grandmother, I created Joy events for my two grandchildren and cheered them on. As a teacher, I encouraged both Joy and discipline in my students, but I contained my own Joy. As a psychotherapist, I celebrated the occasional Joy eruptions in the lives of my clients and kept my Joys private. As a healer, I reined in my Joy because I did not want to stand out or overwhelm others.

When I reviewed my journals from 2009 to 2019, I realized that I had apprenticed to Joy for more than ten years! Sometimes, I crab walked; other times I said a shy "yes." Sometimes I questioned myself about whether my openness to Joy was a spiritual bypass? Gradually, I claimed my entitlement to be a magnet for Joy.

When I first became an apprentice to Joy, I had no idea that transcending the Joy judgments of my culture would require me to break rank with my past cultural conditioning, inter-generational family beliefs, and my own projections and illusions.

Joy commanded my attention—interrupting my sleep and flirting with me during the day. It tickled my imagination and challenged me to resource my Joy genes in my daily life. Gradually, I recovered a dim soul strand that re-awakened me to the reality that eternity yearns for Joy. Then I remembered that the duty of delight is to foster Joy.

Most people understand human evolution in environmental and biological terms. I am aware of another path of human evolution that is nurtured and cultivated by the spiritual awakening of our consciousness. Midway through my seventh decade, I have an inner knowing that Joy and a heightened sense of the sacred may be a seventh sense. Part of my soul agreement is to build awareness and sensitivity to the energy of the sacred. I am convinced that the experience and expression of Joy is integral to sacred awareness.

For five decades I have kept handwritten journals. Writing brings clarity and keeps me honest with myself. In 1999 Alison Strickland and I co-authored *Harvesting Your Journals–Writing Tools to Enhance Your Growth and Creativity*. We had both been devoted journal keepers for more than twenty-five years. My journal is a record of movement and momentum from limited ego identification and Personal Story to becoming more aligned with my authentic self and Soul Story. It is my roadmap and almost always brings me back to my magnetic north, which is connected to my Soul Story.

I returned to my journals to distill deeper meaning and connection by using the following prompts that Alison Strickland contributed to *Harvesting Your Journals:*

I learned
I re-learned
I discovered
I re-discovered
I regret
I appreciate
Right now I feel
And I will

At age seventy-four I experienced that preciousness and Joy were connected. I smile as I remember Susan Tiberghien, author of *One Year to a Writing Life*, saying with her elfish smile, "The footprints of your soul are in your journal." She was right! Have a look!

May 16, 2018

I am a seer and namer. As a namer, words carry both energy and meaning for me. I enjoy creating words like: "Femifesting," "Cosmicity," "Everywhen," and "Inspirited Ones."

I have a talent for sensing what is missing or unexpressed and naming the invisible. When I was a child, I named the unexpressed feelings in my family. Perhaps that is why I was given the nickname "Weenie Witch."

I see between dimensions and beyond physical life. When I show up, I often sense or see what is missing. Part of seeing is naming. When I am in touch with my soul, I see with my inner sight. When I am aligned with sacred awareness, I see truth as well as what is missing or blocked. Seeing is unwrapping denial. My favorite part of seeing is beckoning the future as a place of revelation—not fear.

In March 1977, when my almost fifteen-year-old son, Mike, was electrocuted in the schoolyard next door, I gradually named the invisible realms of grief. I journaled about my feelings and my changing consciousness. My family and friends were stunned when I shared messages about death and the afterlife that I received from my dead son. Although he was dead, he had energy, motion, and intention—just like words! I felt vulnerable and often a bit crazy. Mike was my Wayshower about the continuation of life and the Joy connection. Over time, other "Inspirited Ones" visited with poignant and evidential messages for their loved ones.

Not in my wildest imagination did I plan to write *Healing Grief–A Mother's Story* about my experience with grieving the death of my son. I yearned for stories from other mothers who had survived and re-invested in love after the death of a child. Although Elisabeth Kubler Ross taught about the stages of grief, there were no Mothers' stories available. What a paradox to return to my journals and write the book that I most wanted to read.

I had not expected to write a book about Joy either. Yet once I named the feeling, I recognized that Joy demanded I embody its essence. The paradox of naming the grief journey when I was thirty-three and forty-one years later writing about the stages of Joy bedazzles my mind. Then I entertain myself by wondering if it is possible to be an over-Joyer, which feels to me like the polarity to being an over-giver and over-achiever.

As a student and teacher of women's adult development, I agree that historically we, as women, tend to internalize failure while men tend to internalize success. I am encouraged to write that I believe that we, as women, are liberating ourselves from the internal oppression which has kept too many of us stuck in Personal Story for too long, and we are now honoring connection and community as potential Joy arousers.

Feminine consciousness weaves and interweaves stories in order to shift consciousness. Questions that circled me and commanded my attention as I wove words together into stories included:

How do we, as women, know when we are ripe for a breakthrough or epiphany?

What are our inner signals that catalyze us to claim more of our authentic selves in spite of the insistent chants from the inner and outer chorus to remain safe and honor the status quo?

Who are our midwives of Joy?

What are the messages of Joy that echo back to us from our ancestors and future ancestors?

The Hopi elders believe that we are now in a fast-flowing river and that many of us would be afraid and try to cling to shore. But those who cling to shore will suffer greatly. The advice of the elders was to let go of the shore and push off into the middle of the river. Then look around to see who is there with us and celebrate. I am wondering, what is your relationship to celebration, community, and Joy?

I challenge myself and you to dare to claim or reclaim our Preciousness, Radiance, and Joy. My Invitation: Who might we become if we allowed ourselves to be taken over by Joy? In what ways would our lives and the world be different if we committed ourselves to Joyful creativity and service?

The world needs our visions, our voices, our passion, and our healing wisdom.

CHAPTER 1

Personal Story

"It is love that shows us that the stories of the ego
are not as enticing as we first thought."

~MEGHAN DON

THE DYNAMICS OF PERSONAL STORY

Yes, this is a book about choosing Joy. Yet I choose to begin by writing about Personal Story because I have spent most of my life living under its influence. Yes, and Personal Story is seldom the narrative of Joy.

Stories form us and define our lives. As soon as something happens we create a Story. We are the accumulation of the stories we tell ourselves about who we are and how the world should be. Family, friends, and life itself condition our Stories.

For me, Personal Story is grounded in drama, pain, scarcity, separation, and self-sabotage. However, take heart; the energy will shift and uplift as you move forward and step into your unique Edge-Walking and Soul Stories. Along the journey, expect to experience some Bouncing Stories because the three stories co-exist, and the opportunity to bounce out of and between stories is ever-present.

I believe that Stories carry the elixir of transformation. Like dimensions, Stories co-exist. Each Story has costs and benefits, risks and fulfillment, suffering and Joy. At some point in our spiritual journey, the Story we have been living becomes too small.

I am grateful for the presence of my guides who channeled:

Remember that any time you choose to activate old patterns, you are playing safe.

Over-reaction and suppression also undermine growth.

Growth demands evolving behavior free of fear, denial, and projection.

Like a snake that sheds its skin because it has grown too big, we can choose to create a bigger container. Letting go of limiting beliefs, which are often multigenerational, is the place to begin. As I inquired into my own thoughts, I discovered how attachment to limiting beliefs caused pain, drama, and suffering.

Breaking rank is an evolutionary impulse. Each time I have dared to break rank with limiting beliefs I also had the choice to reclaim parts of myself that I had dimmed over time.

In order to break rank with my versions of intergenerational energy-diminishing beliefs, I had to allow myself to be bigger.

The essential question to wrap your heart and mind around to move out of your Personal Story is: "Who would I have to become to sustain a bigger life?"

Every family has its challenges, secrets, failings, shadows, and inter-generational karma. Without self-awareness and focused intention, we play the roles we learned in our family because we tend to become the person other people defined us as being.

We are all embedded in time and personal history, and that is a trap. Hard-wired habits cast trance-like spells that seduce us to cling to safety and the known. Over-identification with Personal Story can generate exhaustion, emotional bankruptcy, fear, confusion, doubt, and debilitating psychological paralysis. Any one of these states can keep us within the realm of known misery for years, even decades.

Archetypal family wounds cause us to devalue who we are and keep us in a life-dimming Personal Story unless we end the trance or "trance end" our intergenerational wounds and limiting beliefs. The most common archetypal family wounds include:

Abandonment
Abuse
Addiction
Betrayal
Illness
Poverty
Violence

Ego grounds Personal Story and ego is a tyrant. Trance ending ego means refusing to accept the learned limitations of ordinary consciousness. Peeling off limited beliefs, past lifetime vows, and even entities create more energy and deeper truth. Think of an entity as an "uninvited other" that feeds off your energy.

Breaking rank from the limiting beliefs that I adopted as a child required me to challenge my perceptions, projections, and distortions. Letting go of starring in my limited Personal Story required courage and stamina. Breaking rank with the limiting beliefs that I had swallowed and then embodied became my ongoing work. Here's an entry I recorded in my journal more than ten years ago:

December 1, 2009
Breaking rank opened my heart.
Breaking rank caused floods of tears.
Breaking rank honored the promises I made to my soul
　　before I was born.
Breaking rank taught me to honor my own body's knowing.

Breaking rank cost me the conditional love of my family.

Breaking rank was a homecoming to my authentic self—eventually.

THE INVASIVE EGO

Ego rules ordinary awareness and Personal Story. My old ego script that grounded my Personal Story screamed, "Who do you think you are?" when I imagined moving beyond familiar roles. Then my ego screamed, "What if you can't deliver, Missy?" However, when I remembered and chose to align with my Soul Story, my inner voice expanded and exclaimed, "Nonsense! God delivers—not you."

Think about ego, which grounds Personal Story, as forever pointing out where love is missing. Another way to wrap your arms around ego is to experience it as core resistance to the soul. Also, I believe that the existence of the ego is what makes us human. I was comforted when I thought of my egoic self as a lost and wounded child who yearned to go home. Remember that ego operates in linear time and lacks a spiritual perspective. Furthermore, the ego is any aspect of yourself that you have denied, repressed, disowned, or projected—including shame. Remember that ego excels at blaming, accusing, defending, comparing, splitting, and controlling. I agree with Ram Dass, *Be Here Now*, who wrote, "Ego is the soul's karma."

Scarcity and lack are hallmarks of Personal Story. Both the beliefs that "I am not enough" and "I am just enough" align with poverty consciousness. For instance, all the cells in my body went on alert when a woman in one of my writing workshops proclaimed triumphantly, "I finally get it. Being non-orgasmic is connected to scarcity thinking." I find that each time I dare to fire myself from beliefs that had earlier defined and diminished me, I experience that I no longer belong to myself in the ways I always had.

Expect to experience many small ego deaths as you deepen your commitment to move beyond your Personal Story. Shifts from Personal

Story to Edge-Walking Story and from Edge-Walking Story to Soul Story do not happen without resistance.

Consider that we all have two aspects of Self: the scared self and the inviting self. Scared self, which is ego-driven, will convince you that you don't deserve, don't belong, and don't know. When I learned more about my scared self by apprenticing to self-knowledge and self-discovery, I empowered myself to pivot my anxiety and make decisions that were aligned with my inviting self. Each time I chose inviting self, I loosened ego's grip and moved toward my Edge-Walking Story.

In 2011, my guides channeled this about ego:

Your ego is a place of pain, suffering, and separation. Wherever you cling, you create pain and suffering for yourself and others.

If you deny the existence and impact of ego, it will fight back harder to survive.

Becoming more aware of your divinity disconnects you from pain and suffering.

To say that the ego is not divine implies it comes from elsewhere—but from where?

When you look underneath all the desires of the ego, you will understand that ego is looking to be loved.

All is the Beloved.

After that channeling, I experienced a huge AHA moment and realized that, similar to shadow, the ego is core resistance to awakening to our authentic self and stepping into our Edge-Walking or Soul Stories. Then it seemed natural that to break my attachment to ego, I needed to befriend it because I had experiential evidence that self-acceptance and self-love dissolve ego. One of the strategies I used to befriend ego was to imagine sitting in a comfortable rocking chair as a grandmother rocking my ego back and forth in a nurturing manner.

Answering the following question helps me to clarify which Story I am acting in: "Which self am I affirming by my thoughts, feelings, and actions: frightened self or inviting self?"

I agree with Laurel Clark, *The Law of Attraction,* who wrote: "Every physical habit starts with a thought. When you are attached to an idea, it becomes part of you." Stay out of your head when you are embedded in your Personal Story. It's a bad neighborhood.

Picture this scene: I am swimming and floating in Etna Pond at summer's beginning—visiting the lily fields alive with half-opened white and yellow blossoms, their underwater slender roots tickling my feet and legs. Patches of cold water surprise me and take my breath away. I am alone on this lake with no houses visible. The sun is high in the cloudless sky. Green forests surround the blue water. Gratitude and deep contentment are all I know or remember knowing.

Even when I heard the train coming near, I remained relaxed. It passed by and then I heard the loud screech of brakes. Then I watched the engineer cup his hands to his mouth and bellow, "Didn't anyone tell you it is dangerous to swim alone?"

My body shuddered as if I had sustained a physical blow. Instinctively, I shouted back, "Do you notice that I am not telling you how to drive your train?"

For a few flickering moments I felt justified for standing up for myself. Then I remembered to breathe and looked at the beauty that surrounded me. And my heart opened wide again. No question that my passionate, sarcastic reaction was a signal that I was triggered and had bounced from my Soul Story smack into my Personal Story within seconds. I felt remorse and hoped that I would have the opportunity to apologize to the man driving the train. Later that evening I decided to return to my journal to go deeper into the event.

July 8, 2019

ME: Why did you come to me?

ENGINEER: I noticed you swimming by yourself for a few days and I was concerned about your safety. Swimming alone is dangerous.

ME: Yes, and I am a strong swimmer. I swim almost every day, and I enjoy swimming alone sometimes because I don't have to talk to anyone, and I can inhale the beauty of the water, the wind, the lilies, and the sky.

ENGINEER: As long as you are safe. That's all I was concerned about.

ME: My safety never enters my mind when I swim alone. Perhaps that is because I believe that I have lived as a mermaid during several lifetimes.

ENGINEER: Maybe so, but this lifetime you are a human woman and I again remind you that swimming with a buddy is safer than swimming solo. Think of me as your life preserver.

ME: Thank you for your concern. I am sorry I went off on you. I am not accustomed to strangers caring.

ENGINEER: Toot Toot!

And the train continues to clickety-clack down the tracks.

PERCEPTIONS AND BELIEFS

The shift from Personal Story to Edge-Walking Story requires adopting a different perspective. For me, that means substituting the question "Why is this happening FOR me?" in place of "Why is this happening TO me?" Another question that distances me from my limiting Personal Story is, "Who do I desire to become?"

I believe we create our own reality, and that means our outer life is an expression of our inner world. How I make meaning out of an event is at the heart of each Story. Why? Because my perception of the event and consequent meaning-making is based on my past experiences, and some of my past associations are not even conscious!

Sometimes we are so caught up in the trance of our small Personal Story that we fail to be aware of both the inner and outer signals that invite us to break free of our limited Personal Story and risk the unknown. Even synchronistic events have no impact. We are caught in our own spell.

My sense of control is grounded in my need to know. When I own my pattern of needing to know and expect myself to know everything effortlessly, my perception of myself, others, and the world, change. Granted, as a first-born child and grandchild, I was expected to excel. However, when I remember to align with a larger perspective, I also am convinced that my parents' expectations mirrored a belief about my own high expectations which I brought in this lifetime.

In my experience, we only perceive what we believe exists. This concept is important because beliefs underlie which Story we inhabit. Also, beliefs have consequences that can inhibit our intuitive knowing and our spiritual growth. When I took responsibility that the life I am in the process of creating or reacting to is an out-picturing of my most predominant beliefs, I worked full time uprooting limiting beliefs.

It is possible to become addicted to our most cherished beliefs because limiting beliefs offer a sense of certainty. As I broke rank with my limited beliefs, I discovered how my attachment to my limiting beliefs caused pain, drama, and suffering to others and myself.

Seldom do I see the whole picture, especially when my ego is directing my perceptions, feelings, and reactions. For example, take a look at how my ego acted out in this situation.

April 10, 2018
I first noticed several men wearing black leather Hell's Angels jackets sipping coffee as I waited for my plane flight

from Norfolk, Virginia, to Bangor, Maine. I shivered as I remembered being in my mid-thirties and afraid to drive to my office in the Old Port district in Portland, Maine, because the Hell's Angels motorcycle group had "taken over" the area. Instantly, as if my consciousness was updating itself, I also remembered that, in past years, members of the motorcycle club collected Christmas presents for children. The two memories collided in my consciousness.

I was not surprised that my seat on the plane was next to one of the men that I observed at the airport. He stood up when I signaled him that the middle seat was mine. I was dressed in goddess garb—a long, flowing teal skirt and round, glistening moonstone earrings.

A few tense minutes went by. I wondered if he had labeled me, too. On impulse, I asked, "Are you as uncomfortable sitting beside me as I am being your seatmate?"

He smiled and replied, "Yes, maybe even more."

Then he continued, "Say, have you ever ridden a bike?"

"Yes, in Bali, Indonesia, on a rainy day. The one-lane dirt road was wet and slippery. I skidded and fell off the seat and I have never ridden a motorbike since."

"Didn't the person who rented you the bike tell you how to meet your bike before you sat down on the seat?"

"What do you mean?" I asked.

"Every experienced biker makes friends with his bike by saying, 'Thanks for a safe journey,' before switching on the ignition."

"Thanks for the tip," I said sincerely. "I will remember 'to meet' the bike if I ever ride one again."

Then he smiled and asked casually, "What do you do for a living?"

"I do soul readings."

"Tell me about that," he said seriously. "I mean I've never met anyone who admits to reading souls," and we both laughed.

"Oddly enough, it's similar to how you described meeting your bike."

Spontaneously, we gave each other a high five and then leaned back in our assigned seats and enjoyed silence for the remainder of the flight to Maine. I smiled to myself as I realized that I had broken rank with another limiting belief. Then I sighed and giggled as I remembered that Joy is peace resting and I was resting well.

I learned that I lose out when I label people.

I re-learned that when I get out of my own way, there is more that connects us than separates us.

I felt uncomfortable and put off initially. After our conversation I felt a sense of relief and surprise.

I appreciated that both the biker and I dared to move out of our personal prejudices to discover our mutual connections.

And I will remember to be more present for whatever emerges without allowing my past experiences to determine my actions.

Limited thinking, a hallmark of Personal Story, is often grounded in doubt, guilt, and fear. Whenever I am aware of thinking or saying, "How terrible, how painful, or how stupid," I know that I run the risk of sinking into fear and distancing myself from being aware of a larger perspective. When I over-gave and knocked my emotional boundaries off balance, I felt guilty and then resentful until I figured out that resentment is a manifestation of fear.

Another way I keep myself in Personal Story is by being over-patient and over-giving. It is a skill that I have practiced and refined over lifetimes. As I disentangled myself from my Personal Story, I realized that I serve nobody by patiently listening to woe tales that are ego-driven. While harvesting my journals I recovered this example of how easy it is to get lost in Personal Story.

August 13, 2019

I shake my head at a conversation I had with an older Maine woman. She complained, "Imagine how you would feel if more than seventeen people invaded your house."

I replied in a casual voice that she did not have to put up with that kind of ruckus if she chose not to.

She pointed her finger at me and shook her head from side to side and sputtered, "How dare you tell me to leave my own home. I could never do that."

I took a step backward, breathed, and reminded myself good-naturedly that this was not my problem.

Then she muttered, "Nothing will ever change."

I smiled and agreed with her because I know that we create our reality based on our most persistent belief. I was clear that I did not plan to join her in being a victim. I decided to be silent about reminding her she was allowed to not put up with that ruckus and to not leave her own home. If she chose to be silent, nothing would ever change. I knew I was not responsible for her. Then I shook her hand and left. As I walked away, I congratulated myself on setting my own boundary.

FEELINGS AND FREQUENCIES

Remember, that in an energetic universe, it's all about vibration. You cannot vibrate at your peak when you are stuck in Personal Story. Energy can move as quickly as your imagination. Quantum physics suggests that any consistent feeling creates an energy field surrounding your entire body called a torus, which attracts all with which it resonates. To create energetic coherence, thoughts, feelings, and actions must match to create clarity. Following through with right action is the next step.

Both conscious and unconscious patterns have a negative impact. When I am stuck in Personal Story, unresolved emotional wounds surface as self-sabotage whenever life offers me opportunities to prosper. Remember that the roles we play are developmental, and we have different perspectives relative to what roles we play: daughter, sibling, career, partnership, friend, parent, and grandparent. Perspective shifts as we move from Story to Story. Here's the good news—once we learn the lessons, the roles are no longer necessary.

Soul growth requires that I feel my own feelings, pierce through my projections and obsessions, and own every emotion so my buried feelings no longer own me. If I don't do my emotional work, I am taking up too much space on this planet. I often fantasized about screaming: "Break out. Break free. Break your inner vows that no longer serve you. Break through. Break up. Break loose."

From a spiritual perspective, self-doubt, fear, lack, or self-sabotage are truly opportunities to heal. We are always at a choice point! Breaking rank with the limiting beliefs that cement us in Personal Story creates a pathway out of Personal Story. I posted this quotation by Terry Tempest Williams, *When Women Were Birds*, to each mirror in my home: "I am going beyond my own conditioning—breaking rank with what was breaking me."

Because I am an empath, I feel the feelings and emotions of the people around me. Unless I consciously pull my energy back from the energy of low vibrational Personal Stories, I remain a victim. Many years ago, my guides suggested a simple strategy to return to my own energy field: "Repeat your social security number."

Remember that experience depends on frequency. The frequency of pain, guilt, self-condemnation, resentment, cynicism, and fear are all low frequencies. Pain results from holding on to limiting beliefs and keeps us hostage to our Personal Story. A need to be in control creates contraction and lowers our frequency. According to the principles of Future Pull, pain often pushes until future pulls.

For example, consider how the following channeling created momentum for me to move out of my Personal Story:

You did not come here to be accepted.

Your approval for yourself is an extension of your soul.

Dare to step into the larger picture of who you are as well as who you are becoming.

Right now.

My guide's words thundered through every cell of my body.

I gasped, exhaled, and tentatively felt into the frequency that my guides had created. My soul recognized truth. Then I sighed deeply, acknowledging that I had wasted decades of my life pleasing people, by being obedient to the beliefs of others, shape shifting myself to fit in and being the person people expected me to be, contorted myself into many chameleon lookalikes—all to gain approval, love, and a sense of belonging.

The next day, I returned to the prompts and wrote:

I learned how I responded to truth in my physical body.

I felt hopeful that I was capable of validating myself despite my history of shape shifting myself to fit in.

And now I will practice listening to my body's signals as I learn how to come home to my own truths without expecting myself to do this perfectly.

GROWING AND EXPANDING AWARENESS

Self-awareness and will determine which Story we star in. If we become entrenched in our limited Personal Story, we can convince ourselves that we lack awareness and experience in knowing how to bridge into more expansive stories. The tension between Personal narrative, Edge-Walking narrative, and Soul narrative is ongoing. That is how we evolve. Stories have an agenda. There is a difference between our personal agenda and our soul's agenda.

Tracking my ten-year apprenticeship to Joy in my journals, I discovered that the key question that determined which Story I inhabited was: "Does this thought or action align with scarcity, fear, and drama or with discernment, empowerment, abundance, and Joy?" Taking action is the next step.

No matter what the circumstances, being aware is the natural antidote to trance living. The more aware I am, the less I project. To maintain faith in myself, no matter how much my confidence may annoy some people, I choose to maintain a high level of self-awareness while also being aware of the world around me. If I dim-down my awareness, I am ripe to be hooked by my Personal Story. Once again, I returned to my journals to find an example and discovered this Story.

May 29, 2018

I had just snuggled into my beach chair and applied sunscreen. I closed my eyes because the sun was bright and I had forgotten my hat. I was on the precipice of beginning to do a gratitude meditation when I jumped up from my chair, drenched with water!

I opened my eyes and a young woman from Australia introduced herself and apologized for her son's behavior. Then she took his hand, bent down to his height, and said firmly, "Awareness, James, Awareness."

I was touched by her three-word call to attention. No

14

reprimands or shaming—only awareness. I wished I had raised my children and grandchildren with that respectful and kind principle.

About an hour later, I was stung twice by jellyfish while swimming. If I had been aware, I would have stayed out of the water. And I smiled at myself as I whispered, "Awareness, Rosalie, Awareness."

I re-learned that awareness could be nurtured and modeled.

I felt grateful for my sense of humor.

I appreciated the mother's generosity of spirit.

I also appreciated my capacity to adopt a new way of being in relationship that felt self-affirming rather than self-negating.

My guides blessed me with their perspective.

July 19, 2015
Guides:
Remember that becoming conscious requires awareness, intention, and action.

Lean into the present moment as if that is all there is.

Invite all of your senses to participate in this moment.

Merge with leisure.

Appreciate all that surrounds you.

Laugh for no other reason than pleasure.

Savoring leads to deeper contentment.

Research indicates that curiosity improves memory and general brain functioning, and wonderment reduces pessimistic beliefs that support helplessness and trigger a weak immunity. I am curious about the difference between observation and judgment. I have a hunch that self-judgment keeps me in Personal Story and that self-observation opens possibilities for me to engage my Edge-Walking narrative. What I do know for sure is that when I am in judgment, I am not available to witness. Once again, I am grateful for my guides who offered the following counsel:

December 1, 2009

Balance and harmony are essential elements of being centered.

Growth demands evolving behavior free of fear, denial, and projection.

Over-reaction and suppression also undermine growth.

Practice replacing fear by the love of discovery.

ROLES AND LINEAGE

Along the journey, I grew to appreciate how our identities are all learned. For example, closing down or being less than I am was a role I learned as a child. My mother was jealous of me long before I had words. My maternal grandmother loved me unconditionally. To remain safe in my family, I perfected the art of being just enough, seldom too much. Yet, even when I diminished myself, I still threatened my mother.

Women in my lineage did not believe they were important. They also judged their own needs as not valid. Both my mother and her mother diminished themselves in relationship to men and authority figures. The only kind of love that counted in my family was sacrificing self for the needs of others—especially other family members.

At a recent International Women's Writing Guild (IWWG) conference, I wrote the following statements that represented breaking rank with some of my mother's limiting beliefs:

I will not sacrifice my dreams because I value security.

I will not boast an immaculate house at the expense of my creativity and other delights.

I will not refuse to stand up for my daughter.

I will not appear in public as a looking-good family.

I will not pretend that my marriage is perfect.

I will not choose a favorite child or grandchild.

I will not fail to apologize when I am confronted and find that I am at fault.

THE POWER OF INTENTION

To counteract the habit of sacrificing my own needs and ultimately myself, I set an intention to choose myself each day. Setting an intention is essential because the act of declaring an intention gives direction to our unconscious mind. In my experience, I have come to know that we form our world by our intention and we hold our world together by attention.

Writing intentions in my journal and then posting them on mirrors and my refrigerator adds momentum.

September 18, 2014
I choose what I bless with my energy.

I choose whom I will invite into my world and my confidence.
I choose to love outrageously.

I choose to be open to beauty, humor, service, mystery, and grace.

When I set my intention to be more self-loving, I became aware of how I judged myself. Then self-doubt popped up! Both of my reactions felt powerful and well-entrenched. Then I re-directed my attention back to inviting self.

April 5, 2018

Not sure why I have chosen to integrate two massive downloads in the last two years by getting sick. I admit that a recent illness was a direct response to my announcing that I wanted to add another day of reflection to my week. However, when I said that, I had no idea how that was going to happen. Yet, within five hours I was sick and ultimately canceled five days of work! It took that dramatic of an event for me to commit to being more conscious of my words. However, last night I acknowledged how hard I push myself to DO and I took responsibility for being more aware of what was "just enough" because that resonates with Personal Story.

I re-learned that words are energetic magnets, and I need to be mindful of the words I think and speak.

I re-learned that illness could be an opportunity to examine personal beliefs and choose life affirming beliefs and behaviors.

I felt the physical, mental, and emotional impact of my addiction to over doing.

I appreciated that abundance is the attractor in Soul Story.

And I will create dedicated time to relax and enjoy.

Interesting that my sojourn into illness happened about the same time as June Bro's article in *Venture Inward* magazine about me and my book *Living Future Pull*. I did not know what to do with her praise of both the book and me. I hid. That's when I realized that my ego is in charge when I do not allow myself to receive praise!

Tiredness often results from feeling like a victim and being stuck in Personal Story. Sometimes the question is not "What is life?" but rather, "How alive is life?"

According to Sam Keen, *To Love and Be Loved,* "Nothing shapes our journeys through life so much as the questions we ask."

In the process of harvesting a decade of my journals, I identified a handful of questions that clarified some of the elements of my limited and limiting Personal Story. Have a look.

Journal Entries
2009 through 2019

Where is the place of drama, lack, or scarcity in my life?

What are my most familiar coping patterns?

How much stress do I cause myself by self-criticism?

Where do I play life the safest?

What inherited beliefs keep me limited?

What are my most repeated victim stories?

Who or what demands allegiance?

What stories am I attracting, repelling, and co-creating?

KARMA CLEAR

Month after month I wrote about the place of karma within the framework of stories. Eventually, I felt comfortable knowing that suffering lifetime after lifetime is not the purpose of karma. Karma is meant to be resolved, not accumulated. Then I tripped on a quotation by John C. Lilly, *The Center of the Cyclone*, "Burning karma is making conscious the consequences of your past actions without shame, anger, or censoring." The process of releasing karma is the act of taking responsibility. Releasing karma affects future personality as well as the past one.

April 16, 1999

I knew I needed to travel to Cyprus, but I had no clue why. When the plane landed, I felt anxious. And I continued to feel anxious for most of the sixteen days we visited. I knew in advance that the country was partitioned and that an uneasy peace was kept in place by UN Peacekeepers. Even that did not explain the depth of my anxiety.

Several people told us we must visit a particular castle. My body screamed, "No." Twice we were en route to the castle and I got physically ill. I recognized my resistance and decided to surrender even though every cell in my body wanted me to run away. As soon as my feet touched down on the castle grounds, I felt bereft and breathless. I had no logical explanation for my emotions.

The tour guide was friendly and spoke English. He looked surprised when I told him I needed to visit the third floor where the ladies-in-waiting resided in the past. He nodded his head and said with a wink, "Most people don't know about that."

I knew with every cell in my body that I was about to be seized by a past life karmic memory and I made a firm intention to remember all the details so I could integrate the bleed-through lifetime. Then I felt nauseous, and I knew the energetic memory was real.

When we reached the top step, I regressed 400 years and I saw, with my inner eyes, my former 16-year-old ardent and attractive self. I was a lady-in-waiting to the queen. More memories flooded my consciousness. I remembered my love for the queen and the voluntary vow of faithfulness I made to her. As I looked around at the familiar furniture and the colorful walls surrounding me, I remembered the king who was fifteen years older than his 28-year-old wife. My body shook as I remembered how I had kept my distance from him because I knew he was attracted to me.

The next scene appeared, and I remembered the day when all the court, except for the Queen, went on a hunting party. The king cut me off from the rest of the ladies and ordered his men to go on ahead, leaving him and me alone. I screamed for help. Nobody came. I fought. He was strong. Eventually, he had his way, assuring me that he had loved me since I had arrived in court.

I was devastated and blamed myself for betraying the trust of the queen. Under the cover of darkness, I fled the castle undetected. I dared not return to my family because I believed that I had disgraced not only myself but also my family. I wandered for days without food or water. I dared to travel only at night, hiding from the king and his men because he vowed to pursue me. After many lonely months of wandering, I died.

I learned how body memories span lifetimes.

I re-learned how my intuition leads me to embrace bleed through past lifetimes in order to heal.

I felt devastated and guilty and ready to forgive myself for being unable to keep my vow to the queen.

I regret that my sexuality has been my shadow this lifetime until now.

And I will do a healing ritual and reclaim my innocence.

After recording the above trauma in my journal, I went deeper in order to heal. Two themes that have shadowed me most in this lifetime are over-giving to prove that I am trustworthy and a tendency to with-hold compassion from myself. I knew instinctively that self-forgiveness was a healing antidote to self-judgment, and I did a ritual and forgave myself and then blessed myself.

Sometimes it takes a jolt to bounce us out of our Personal Story. Illness and loss often serve as messages from Future Pull and assist us in moving out of Personal Story. My most recent example of sinking back into my diminishing Personal Story is when I felt anxious, fearful, and vulnerable about upcoming cataract surgery. I could not talk myself out of dreading the surgery.

Many of my friends told me to get over myself and shared their successful surgery stories. My daughter, an anesthesiologist, offered to assist the eye doctor. I judged myself as weak and a coward and sunk into shame and then judged myself.

Imagine my surprise when an angel intervened and tutored me about self-compassion. Her intervention swept me out of my Personal Story. This was a perfect example of pain pushing until future pulls. I will return to this story in later chapters as I deepened my awareness about why the eye surgery threatened to overwhelm me.

SELF LOVE

Love moves us out of Personal Story and into Edge-Walking Story and Soul Story. To move out of Personal Story, I choose to strengthen new ways of being that include self-love and self-worth while tolerating uncertainty and entertaining the future as a place of revelation rather than fear. Also, I challenge myself daily to have as much faith in things that are fading away as things that are growing.

I enjoy affirming that more is always emerging. One way to evaluate which Story is working in us is to discern if life is more and more satisfying. Also, be prepared to challenge yourself with the question: "Am I okay to be okay?"

Our soul constantly calls upon our ego to die to its illusions. There is an energetic difference between allowing, affirming, and claiming. As I recognize and break rank with my learned limitations, I become more aware of my Joy potential.

September 15, 2017

I know I have choices in how I shape the future. I vow to examine my beliefs and ongoing thoughts to support moving into the future with vision and courage because I know from experience that a belief is a thought I keep thinking.

I yearn to be beyond connecting my sense of spiritual and human self-worth on how many readings I do in a month. I want to expect prosperity. What might happen, I wonder, if I make an intention to believe that all I wish to Femifest is already mine?

SUGGESTIONS FOR MOVING OUT
OF PERSONAL STORY
Harvested From My Journals

Feel your feelings.

Rid yourself of over functioning and under functioning behavior.

Affirm, "I count."

Release assumptions and judgments.

Replace fear with curiosity.

Sever beliefs that resonate with drama, lack, mediocrity, separation, and learned limitations.

Create healthy emotional and physical boundaries.

Banish gossip and negative thinking.

Identify and release life negating internal dialogue.

Release all aspects of self-judgment, self-rejection, and self-hatred.

Heal Integrity Breaches (lies, withheld truths, and broken agreements).

CLIFF NOTES TO SELF: PERSONAL STORY

Wherever we put our attention is where we put our power.

Uncertainty is one of the most essential ingredients to learn to tolerate and embrace.

We are separate from Source only for as long as we think we are separate.

How I treat myself is an example to the world of how the world should treat me.

The emotional dramas of others are not relevant to my living an authentic life.

If criticism hurts me, it means I am defending myself against it, and I am in my Personal Story.

Guilt is resentment turned against self.

Remember that any time I activate limiting habits, patterns, and beliefs that are aligned with playing safe or honoring the status quo, I am starring in Personal Story.

The ego will clamor loudest when I am on the threshold of transformation.

Happiness requires a certain surrender.

When I limit myself, I limit God.

REFLECTIVE QUESTIONS FOR PERSONAL STORY

Take a breath. Take note of yourself by reading through the following prompts and use the extra space under each item to write about whatever arises from your heart, gut, or soul.

Who and what calls you to break rank?

What do you need to outgrow? What do you need to grow into?

Whose approval matters?

What are you loyal to and why?

To whom do you listen deeply and why?

What if you believed that everything that happened to you is for your own good?

QUOTATIONS FOR REFLECTION

"Most people prefer the certainty of misery to the
misery of uncertainty."
~Virginia Satir

"You are either a host for God or a hostage to your ego."
~A Course in Miracles

"A mind released from self-obsession and limiting beliefs
is freed for fascination, for wonder, for love."
~Catherine Ingram

"In difficult times, you should always carry something beautiful
in your mind."
~Blaise Pascal

"And the day came when the risk to remain tight in a bud
was more painful than the risk it took to blossom."
~Anais Nin

"Strong is what we make each other. Until we are strong together,
a strong woman is a strongly afraid woman."
~Marge Piercy

"When you change the way you look at things,
the things you look at change."
~Chris Griscom

"All boredom has to do with disconnection from self."
~Marx Planck

"The antidote to exhaustion is wholeheartedness."
~David Whyte

NOTES TO SELF

CHAPTER 2

Edge-Walking Story

"Our story is our way home."

~Brene Brown

THE DYNAMICS OF EDGE-WALKING STORY

Living the tension between Personal Story and Edge-Walking Story is an art. Edge-Walking is the bridge between Personal Story and Soul Story. Freedom is liberation from Personal Story. I worked hard to bring fragments of my life together.

The movement from starring in my Personal Story to taking up residence in my Edge-Walking-Story required:

Shifting from being in control to being receptive.

Shifting from over-giving to being centered in my own energy.

Shifting from wanting to know to discovering.

Shifting from wanting validation from others to affirming myself.

Shifting from achieving to enjoying.

Shifting from "Why did this happen to me?" to "If not for_____, I would not _____."

For example:

If not for my two-year apprenticeship to pleasure and leisure, I would not know that I could learn to relax.

If not for my son's death, I would not have personally experienced the reality of my ability to communicate across dimensions.

To move from Personal Story into Edge-Walking Story, be prepared to examine your personal beliefs about whom you are supposed to be and how the world was supposed to work as well as how others were supposed to relate to you. Also, expect to encounter buried pain and buried wisdom.

Taking up residency in Edge-Walking Story requires an active disengagement from learned, limited habits of the past. Radical honesty is essential to make the transition. Courage and community support are necessary. To dare to be awake means to dare to speak your truth, even if you do not know the whole truth.

When we are more aware and more present, our Edge-Walking potential will demand more attention. Since we all were born with free will, we may crab walk around the invitation until our attraction to evolve expands beyond our fear. The key is being present moment to moment.

Consider adding the word "coddiwomple" to your vocabulary and adopt this Edge-Walking way of being: to travel purposefully toward an as yet unknown destination.

Future Pull is a catalyst for transforming. Think of Future Pull as a wild card that invites us to move out of our comfort zone and risk becoming more authentic. Answering the call of Future Pull aligned me with a more trusting, loving, empowering, and compassionate aspect of myself.

I invite you to wrap your arms around Future Pull as a feed-forward event in the present with meaning that unfolds in the future. It is the frequency of Future Pull that challenges each of us to leave behind our Personal Story and to risk bridging into our Edge-Walking and Soul Stories. Always, we are at a choice point. Transformative events alter both our frequency and our perception.

The dynamics of Future Pull include:

The call is unexpected.

The call makes our life larger and larger.

The message is clear and carries divine authority and power.

You comprehend the message instantly.

Your soul greets the message with a sense of quietude.

The truth that it conveys transcends all words.

Love grounds the message.

My guides added their perspective:

Affirm the frequency of Future Pull as a precious resource.

Establish a strong connection with Inspirited Ones.

Embrace your potential and honor your own journey.

Remember that Wonder opens dimensional doorways.

Harvesting my journals brought surprises. Looking back, I spotted the invitation of Future Pull, and I appreciated how clues to my emerging Future Self beamed out from my journal entry. Think feed-forward instead of feed-back.

The following journal entry affirms my intention to be in my light.

June 18, 2011
My new choice was to "power up" my heart when I approached book buyers to stock my most recent book, *Awaken: Awaken Your All Knowing Heart.* I practiced connecting heart-to-heart with the decision-makers. Yesterday I cried with a bookstore

owner when he shared his Story about how he planned to write his own book "someday." I felt his pain and remained in my heart while I encouraged him to write his book now.

Sometimes my role in grounding a Future Pull call manifests over night. Other times, the inner work needed to challenge embedded beliefs takes more time, risk, and courage.

The recurring question that propelled me to do a vision quest and spend three days and nights in May 2013 on the sacred Blue Mountain in Taos, New Mexico, was: "Am I being true to the deepest part of myself?" My intention was to move out of unconsciousness, which is an aspect of personal story, into consciousness, which is an attribute of Edge-Walking and Soul Story.

When the Mama bear and her two cubs appeared about ten feet from my prayer circle on the first night, I was afraid I would not survive. I experienced layers and layers of fear. Every single Davy Crockett movie that I had seen as a kid whizzed through my mind. Eventually, I chose to let go of my fear and panic in preparation for death because I did not want to die feeling overwhelmed by fear or anger. When I opened my eyes, my three visitors were no longer present.

The following day when the Mama bear and her two cubs returned, I surprised myself by "taking up the gaze." Instead of seeing her as a threat to my survival, I beheld her beauty and the round contours of her body. When I merged my energy with hers, I felt imbued with beauty, love and Joy. I noted to myself that I had transformed a deep fear and remained in awe of how perception creates consciousness.

During the vision quest, I received a Spirit message that it was time for me to step into a leadership role. Most of my life I have enjoyed being a teacher. Actually, until this experience, I had always believed I was a born teacher and many people consider me a gifted teacher. For sure, that is when I am actively in touch with my intuition, creativity, compassion, and Joy.

The one predictable result of a breakthrough is a clear inner knowing that I will not return to my former self. Personal history gets erased. Self-consciousness, too, disappeared. God-gasps (Oh my God) erupted between my lips daily and I understood co-creating in a whole different way. My cells felt entrained to a more spacious potential. Best of all, I felt ready and worthy to co-create with God.

I required silence and alone time in order to integrate my cry for vision experience. I gave myself permission to be without words because I discovered that the act of naming limited my experience. I settled for describing my inner process to close friends by saying that my consciousness had altered, like after the first time making love.

Time-out was not ruled by calendar time. I let go of making sense of the experience because my logical mind did not speak the language of reverence. Since I am not a mystic, I do not have the language to describe epiphany. Being convinced that all was in Divine Right Order—including my own life—was my ever-present reality. I longed to rest in the love of God. Returning to myself, God, and silence felt like a basic need.

I returned from the vision quest with a deeper consecration to my journey as well as a deeper sense of vulnerability. Also, I surprised myself with a deeper trust in the invisible alchemical soul process. I was no longer a hostage to ordinary reality.

The time had come for me to expand my role beyond being a teacher to being a spiritual leader. I did not know at the time that I held a limited perspective of leadership in my mind that included hard work but did not include Joy. Cultural beliefs caught me off guard. Mostly, I associated leadership with politics and men. The idea of being a healing leader was not in my consciousness.

When I ended my resident grandmother status in June 2013, I acknowledged that I could easily return to my teaching career. However, when I was honest about my feelings, I admitted to myself that role had little passion for me today. I could also expand my publishing company by publishing and promoting books of friends. Although I enjoy writing, I have little energy for the publishing and promotional aspects of the book trade.

Even when I wrote and published *Soul Befriending* in 2014 and *Living Future Pull* in 2017, I resisted the idea that spiritual leadership might be a Future Pull call. Yet leadership has been part of my life evidenced by teaching in the Advanced Leadership program at the Creative Problem Solving Institute at NYU for more than twenty years!

The call toward leadership would not go away. The Spirit message was a freeze frame in my mind and the call to leadership returned at the oddest moments. Without closing my eyes, I remembered the temperature, the smells of the nearby pine trees, the cold, hard ground that became my bed—even the name of the horse, Gizmo, who delivered me up the mountain.

Intention took on an expanded meaning. I created the concept of "Femifesting" as a way of grounding my expanded relationship to intention. Femifesting acknowledged my relationship to Spirit while manifesting felt limited to my ordinary mind. Words matter to me and "mani" is of the hands while "femi" is of the Spirit. Femifesting linked body and spirit.

The roles of teacher and spiritual leader feel energetically different to me. My soul feels more attuned with the healing path than the teaching path. Yet I also recognize that whatever inner work I have focused on comes to fruition when I teach. That was not always true. However, when I am naked in my honesty, embracing my healing and leadership potential is where growth and Joy reside for me.

To gain more clarity, I returned to the prompts:

I learned that I always have a choice.

I re-learned that surrender does not mean death.

I felt awed by the depth of my connection to the Mama bear when I witnessed her beauty and preciousness.

I appreciated that my cry for vision was honored.

And I will be on the lookout for leadership opportunities, because I believe that when I am not living on my edge, I am taking up too much room on our planet.

GROUNDING INTENTION

It is important to acknowledge exactly where we are when we step into our Edge-Walking Stories. For me, that meant being aware of my longings as well as how I might sabotage myself. In perfect timing, my massage angel, Victoria Beales, shared with me how she fired herself from being a problem solver when she realized that she attracted people with problems to herself because she specialized in solutions. Next, she set an intention to be in the world as a harmonizer. Now she attracts people who seek and value harmony.

I followed her example and broke rank with identifying myself as a light worker and set my intention on Facebook as a light beamer! I am delighted to be a magnet to attract people who want to amplify their light. The unexpected bonus is that I have broken rank with my addiction to work hard!

The greater the transformational potential, the stronger the ego will clamor. Illness tends to be a trigger for me. My inner imperative to BE STRONG feels like part of my core identity, and I do not feel in control of my life when I am sick. At times, illness serves as an agent of Future Pull to wake me up.

January 18, 2017

First entry in more than a week. Several days with the flu left me with no energy to write. Crazy dreams, sometimes waking myself up talking in a strange language with someone or something from outside this dimension. In that "space-time" I understood both parts of the conversation but when I bounced back to ordinary reality, I had no memory.

35

This was the second time in my life that I am aware that I had the choice to live or continue to evolve without a physical body. The first time, when I was bitten by the brown recluse spider, I was out of body and thought I had died already. This time I was fully in my body and still waited for a signal. Both times I waited for a signal that would inform me about the right choice.

Ordinarily, sleep is my time for integration. Sleep deprivation sucks. The sinus drainage in my throat kept me awake and my lungs filled up when I slept. One morning I woke myself up gagging and coughing uncontrollably until I wondered if this was my dying time and questioned if I was struggling against the inevitable. Spontaneously, I said out loud, "If this is my time, I am ready. Take me."

Then I waited. I experienced a mixed feeling of peace and detachment when I understood that both life and death contribute to evolution. Simultaneously, I also understood in that shimmery moment that it was Divine will, not my will—that I intended to surrender to.

When living became my conscious choice, my recovery began. I slept all night for the first time in days. My headache went away. My ribs no longer hurt when I coughed. I was able to read.

During my recovery, I practiced loving myself and being present without an agenda. Updating my consciousness by making a conscious intention and then acting on my decision was essential to stay in my Edge-Walking Story.

My persistent ego demands to exert control by knowing every detail about the writing process. Yet I understand more about the organic, evolutionary dynamics of both inspired and down to earth writing. The voice of my ego challenges, "How can you possibly write the last few chapters of your book if you do not have the capacity to remember words?"

I shrugged in response, refusing to be triggered. Maybe I won't finish this book. Maybe this is another call to surrender.

I am surprised with my ease of imagining letting go of a project that I have worked on for years. I smile as I realize once again that paradox lives within the mystery.

The following dialogue with my guides about applying intention to my ongoing writing spoke directly to my heart and mind.

March 16, 2017

GUIDE: *Writing is more than the gaining of knowledge or loving in the abstract.*

Your words transmit a specific wavelength of frequency that is magnetic and aligned with akashic blueprints.

Speaking, living, and writing from a spacious heart invite wisdom that is distilled from experience.

When you imagine yourself as an agent of evolutionary consciousness, healing and Joy surround you.

ME: If gathering stories and journal entries for the completion of *Living Future Pull* were all I agreed to do, the assignment would be easier. It's the work of clearing, claiming, and living the principles that challenge me during the day and the night. (Sigh) Then I deliberately stop myself from complaining before I slip into Personal Story.

GUIDE: *Continue to write. Foster your focus. Avoid slipping into self-criticism, for that energetic frequency compromises your energy and your receptivity to behold the whole.*

Instead of focusing on regrets, choose to distill what you have learned. Next, create an intimate relationship with pleasure and leisure until you taste and relish that the two activities are one. Consider this your soul growth challenge.

ME: Thank you for the push. I feel ready to relax and befriend pleasure and leisure because I have missed my playfulness.

THE CHALLENGE OF PLEASURE AND LEISURE

I have not given myself permission to be in a relationship with leisure, although the energies of Future Pull confront me daily. I am deeply aware of my own high expectations as well as early family conditioning that chained me to work hard, work often, and work before relaxation. As an adult, I embodied the Puritan work ethic, and I overachieved to win approval and love. Hard work continues to feel like a frozen habit that I choose to melt.

Last night I acknowledged how hard I push myself to DO. I even worked hard at creating and experiencing pleasure and leisure. I also stumbled over many of my own inner, patriarchal rules to hurry up, keep busy, and be productive. Substituting "sacredizing" for "wasting" is a beginning to breaking rank with my inner Puritan ethics, which are Joy deficient.

May 20, 2016

GUIDE: *You have learned well the earth's ways of working hard. It is one of your inherited family values, and hard work has served you in the past. However, you are living with one foot and a large part of the second foot in the future.*

Yes, granted eternity is timeless, and I speak to you in a way your human self understands. The integration of an open heart and an open mind—informed by Spirit—transforms your relationship with work.

At times leisure and pleasure felt like a rupture to my normal way of being. I wrote often about what to do with an abundance of time.

Relax. How? Empty or fill up. When? Then I questioned if receiving and filling up with pleasure is purposeful? "Of course!" I scream to the oncoming waves.

My guides channeled:

Most humans have anxiety around pleasure.

Imagine pleasure as love of self.

Allow yourself more pleasure in life.

Pleasure links with your soul as long as your chosen pleasure does not dim your light.

July 2016

In honor of pleasure and leisure, I greeted the day with a pre-dawn walk in the dew-drenched grass, meditation, and prayer in my sunny loft, followed by chanting, journaling, and then having a fresh salad concocted from the vegetables in my garden.

I appreciated being wide-awake to leisure! Then I wondered if leisure naturally opens to grace. I am content to live into that answer. I remind myself daily, sometimes hourly, to be content with emptying out without worrying about filling up with work or other commitments. The harmonizing of emptiness and fullness remains a mystery

I marvel at the synchronicity. Following through on the guidance, I decided to treat myself to pleasure and leisure yesterday at Pleasant Pond. A little girl, whom I had seen often this summer, approached me and announced, "I'm almost four." I smiled. Then she reached for my hand and said, "Don't worry; it won't be long before you are four, too." I giggled and we splashed each other like two four-year-olds! I laughed with pleasure! She was my self-appointed teacher for the day.

For the second summer and fall, my assignment in apprenticing to pleasure and leisure continued. A solitary loon became my playmate. Although I have written about how people or events often serve as representatives of Future Pull for one another, I had not experienced that animals can also be emissaries until a lone loon picked me up during the last week of June. Initially, I spotted the loon during my first swim when I recognized his haunting call. Then he disappeared. I was unaware that a loon can swim for fifteen feet underwater. As I swam to shore, he surprised me by popping up about four feet in front of me.

We faced each other; neither of us moved. We continued to stare at one another. For several minutes nothing existed but the loon and me. When I realized that I was holding my breath and gasped, he fluffed his wings and exposed his ample underbelly. Then he settled back in the water and returned my gaze.

I felt like clapping my hands in glee, but I did not want to break the magic of the moment. Then he swam off. When my rapidly beating heart slowed down, I cupped my hands to my mouth and shouted, "I'll be back to swim with you tomorrow."

I woke up several times during the night to the sound of far away loon calls. Several times I was tempted to get up and walk down the rocky, dirt path and over the railroad tracks to the lake, but I resisted my impulse.

The next day I looked up the meaning of loon in the Native American Medicine card deck and was not surprised when I read that loons are symbols of peace, harmony, and generosity. They are also considered to be Divine Messengers.

Almost every day for three months I joined my lake companion. Even though we frolicked together at different times of the day, some days he appeared as if he had waited

for me; other days I vigilantly scanned the lake for him.
Spontaneously, I created a loon greeting by taking a deep
breath and chanting, H-E-L-L-O L-O-O-N three times. I
giggled with glee as my voice echoed around the lake.

Mostly, the loon appeared when I focused on the yellow
and white lotuses, the changing patterns of the clouds, fish
jumping nearby, or a heron outlined against the tall trees.
In fact, when I energetically made an intention to attract
the loon, nothing happened. It was only when I let go of
expectations and surrendered to the beauty that surrounded
me that the loon arrived. Magic was in the air when he
fluttered his wings and alerted me to his presence even when
I was tracking the quartet of eagles flying in circles high over
my head. Clearly, I was not in charge of his appearance or
disappearance.

Gradually, we settled into a rhythm and a pattern as
he swam about two arm lengths on my right side. When I
slowed down, he followed. When I speeded up, he matched
my rhythm. During our swim, I had no thoughts, agendas, or
even fantasies. I was present with the loon, the lake, the sky,
and the trees. My relationship to All That Is felt sacred. Later,
I joked to a friend that I enjoyed more one-to-one time with
my loon friend than many human partners spend with one
another. My vision felt laser sharp and my heart felt
wide open.

One day I did not swim because of the loud thunder. The
next day I was surprised when I stepped into the lake at my
usual spot and spied a slender loon feather on a nearby rock.
I smiled, then cried, and celebrated by doing my version of a
loon dance.

Three weeks before I left my home state of Maine to
return to my adopted state of Virginia for eight months,
the loon surprised me with a friend. I was excited for him.

I nodded to her. She ignored me and continued to swim close to her mate. A week later she left his side and swam about two arm lengths away on my left side. I giggled as I imagined these two magnificent birds were my wings, and with their help I could fly if I desired.

On September 29th, 2018 about three months to the day that I met my loon buddy, I woke up at 2:23 AM, feeling sad because I had not seen my loon friends for the past three days. Then I asked myself if I would have done anything different if I had known on September 26th that the day marked our last swim. I cried as I remembered how joyful I felt when I spotted my two friends swimming towards me. I sang my Hello Loons song loudly and they both flapped their wings as they swam closer. I opened my heart even wider. Spaciousness connected us. I felt as if Nature held the three of us in her embrace.

We swam in the lily pads for a while. Then they accompanied me back to shore. I bowed to them as I stepped foot on shore. They both fluttered their wings as they swam off.

As I recalled our last swim together, I realized that I had no regrets. That awareness felt like a deep healing for me because sudden departures or deaths in the past had filled me with regrets whether the death be a person or a familiar guide leaving without warning or a Goodbye.

I reflected on how hard I had worked last summer to feel limited pleasure and leisure. The summer of 2018 I surrendered and my heart opened wider than my imagination. In the process, I reclaimed my inner and outer joy as I welcomed and rejoiced in beauty and Oneness. Grace followed.

The next day Wachian Welch gave me a message from Spirit at Healing Light Church. He said that the loons wanted me to know that they have a fine memory and will join me again when I return next June. Also, he channeled that they invited me to remember them by feeling their presence in my heart whenever I missed them or felt sad.

I nodded and acknowledged to myself that I knew how to do that because Radiance resided in my heart. By remembering grace and glee, I will connect with my feathered friends in the future.

I re-discovered a deeper appreciation of the interconnection of all.

I regretted nothing.

I felt the presence of spaciousness, grace, and glee.

And I will ever be grateful to my feathered friends for opening my heart even wider.

Honoring my apprenticeship to pleasure and leisure, when I was not swimming, I enjoyed hammering and chiseling a whale's tail out of a 98-pound chunk of industrial sandstone. Nobody told me that industrial sandstone had the strength of granite and marble, and my diamond-studded files were useless. While chipping stone, I reminded myself to cut deeper. Then I laughed because I knew in my bones how everything is connected and I appreciated that the loon reminded me of the pleasures of depth just as the stone challenged me to go deeper. For an instant I recognized that lessons and blessings co-existed and I felt surrounded by the sacred.

March 20, 2017
Today I challenged myself to re-write *Living Future Pull* from a place of the heart. My guides suggested that, rather than pursue the re-write as something to be conquered, I experiment with loving the process and loving myself. Their suggestion made sense, especially since the book is about love.

Surrounding the re-writing process with love excites me, especially since I believe that like attracts like. Imagining love grounding the book makes me feel expansive, hopeful, and open to all the possibilities. I smile to myself as I imagine that I am creating energetic coherence.

Is it my imagination or does the universe eavesdrop and test me when I make an intention? My experience votes for the universe being a teacher.

Another dimension of Edge-Walking Story is being intentional about the impact I have on people. Just as I can be overwhelmed easily with all the energy that is passing through me, others can also be overwhelmed with my energy and my Stories.

July 5, 2018

A spontaneous conversation with an elderly man in a coffee line impacted me for several days. He turned to me in the line and said, "Everyone needs a dream."

I nodded in agreement.

He continued, "Lots of people at my retirement home spend days complaining about their bodies, the food, family troubles, even the weather."

He paused and I nodded again. "I smoked four packs of cigarettes a day and got COPD. Then I woke up, stopped smoking, and threw away the oxygen machine. Now I count my blessings every day instead of cigarettes."

I nodded, thanked him for his timely message, and then told him that he was my angel for the day.

"How's that?" he said and scratched his bald head.

"My brother died a few days ago and I don't think he had a dream. His wife had a dream of building a five-bedroom house so their grandkids could visit. The house was ready to move into three days before he died. But the big house was not his dream. I wonder if he had a dream for himself."

The man reached for my hand and said, "I am sorry for your loss and for him."

I could feel his heart.

Without censoring myself, I asked him, "Do you remember the play *South Pacific* and the song 'Happy Talk?'"

He nodded and grinned. Spontaneously, right there in the middle of the restaurant, we both broke out in song and then added the finger dance that grounded the song. People looked up. Some smiled. Others shook their heads. Nobody covered his or her ears. We finished the song.

"Thank you," I said with a full smile. "I am in the process of deciding how I will live out the remainder of my life. You are a teacher for me, and I promise to cozy up with my dreams."

He smiled. We hugged. When he had picked up his breakfast, he walked over to a table in the corner of the restaurant and joined three other people who eyed me with curiosity. Meeting him in the coffee line felt like a sacred encounter. I did not ask him for his name. An intimate exchange happened and we were both blessed.

When my soul buddy, Linda Harris, re-appeared, she questioned, "What was that? I leave you alone for a minute to go to the bathroom and you have picked up another man?"

"Nope, it was mutual. We picked and perked each other up and my heart feels fuller. Plus, I have challenged myself to set an intention about how I will live the rest of my life in conscious Joy."

Several times yesterday I was in tears. Sometimes it was tears of appreciation, reverence, or being overwhelmed by the enormity of this process of coming home to Joy and myself.

My heart knows that tears are a natural response to the sacred, but tears were not allowed in my family. I learned how to suppress my tears and my feelings as a small child.

Honoring the integrity of my tears is another opportunity to break rank. The next step is letting in the appreciation that others give me when I share my authenticity.

As if some form of cosmic choreography is directing my life, a client once said upon leaving from her soul reading, "I bow to your wisdom." I have a hard time accepting that level of acknowledgment. I am happier saying, "We both have good guides."

Then my guides surprised me when they channeled that failure to receive is connected to the ego and Personal Story. However, I re-affirm that I am committed to being a clear channel, and more and more the voices of my guides and my own inner wisdom voice blend and become one.

What if I dismissed my worst fears and believed that my boldest visions can come true? I cannot dismiss the feeling in my gut that something is about to emerge, and I feel edgy. In the past whenever I have experienced being edgy, the energy was waiting to grow. When I made a conscious intention to believe that the as yet unknown future is a place of revelation, I felt more present than fearful.

In my experience, transformational shifts do not happen without resistance. The principle of co-arising continued to challenge me. I captured the essence of co-arising in my journal.

August 2017

I am aware that the dynamics of co-arising pop up each time I sense that I am on the brink of transformation. For example, I ducked when my guides suggested that I entitle my last book *High Beam Living and Loving*. I resisted because I was not ready to claim that much light. Instead, I chose the title *Soul Befriending* and used *High Beam Living and Loving* as the subtitle. Bargaining is seldom efficient. When the book was published, I admitted to myself that I bounced myself back into Personal Story by refusing to claim High Beam Living and Loving.

Another benefit of journaling is being able to trace and track both growth and stuckness. Have a look!

May 14, 2014

My friend Georgia surprised me with an envelope addressed to Rosalie Emery Great Heart from the Old Orchard Alumni Association. We both giggled at my expanded name. Then I posted the envelope and invitation on my refrigerator.

I have not been invited to an alumni reunion for fifty years because I got pregnant during my senior year in high school and was not allowed to attend classes or the graduation ceremony. I got a GED certificate of completion but I did not get a class diploma. Perhaps that motivated me to graduate from college in three years with high honors! During the decades I learned how to validate myself and let go of the judgments of others. I wondered about the timing and the motivation. I questioned if this was another example of Future Pull or someone had slipped up. I toyed with the idea of attending and then chose to carry on with the life that called to me.

September 2012

I wished that I had a re-set button because I am aware that I missed out on Joy amidst the demands of being a hostess, mother, and grandmother. Getting the kids ready to return to school, putting a birthday party together for Noah, helping everyone adjust to a new routine, and supervising Noah and Malia's friends after school, was too much. I allowed the busyness to tire me out and did not journal or channel although I know from experience that both add to my clarity and focus.

Less than two months later I reclaimed my place in my Edge-Walking Story. Here's how!

November 23, 2012

I count back on my aging fingers that three months have passed since I enjoyed a weekend of surrendering to my own rhythms. Twelve weeks of accommodating to the schedules of family is too much and too long.

Returning to my own natural rhythms feels like grace. Silence, sleep, bathing, reading—all morph into one another.

Today I deliberately chose what appeals to me at each moment.

Although I had committed myself to return to writing, my heart was not engaged. Rather than shaming myself for being irresponsible, I reminded myself that I would return to writing tomorrow because I was determined to continue to nurture myself by filling myself up with pleasure.

Reading was my next delight. What book to choose, since I was in the middle of reading three? No coincidence that Sue Monk Kidd, Joanna Macy, and John O'Donohue were all writing about belonging. I gave in to reading a few chapters from each writer and snuggled up to the little girl within me who delighted in sampling Whitman's chocolates from the Christmas candy box—nibbling but never consuming the whole chocolate. I remember my brother tattling and accusing me of biting the heads off the chocolates and never eating the bodies.

I am learning how to be detached from drama and ego so nothing in the universe has power over me. My guides added their spiritual perspective.

September 26, 2013

Be conscious of both your inner rhythm and outer balance.

Be patient with yourself and those around you.

Be loving of yourself and those around you.

Be understanding of your needs and the needs of those around you.

Be mindful that you are not required to respond to the needs of everyone around you.

TRANSMITTING AND RECEIVING LOVE

Remember that self-love was a free pass out of Personal Story. Learning to ground self-love in my daily life was a discipline and over time a delight.

Self-love builds a bridge between Personal Story and both Edge-Walking and Soul Stories. Practicing discernment begins with being honest about what is life-affirming and what is life negating.

To determine how much self-love I extended to myself weekly, I made a list of what nurtures me. Then I made a strong intention to indulge myself in at least ten self-nurturing activities during each week. My commitment to take action steps was important. My pleasure list included: a walk in the woods, tending my garden and inside plants, cooking with my grandchildren, pedicures, improvisational movement, visiting an art museum, playing in the mud. My gratitude was huge.

I am beginning to understand that some of us choose our parents to break rank with restrictive beliefs this lifetime. As I age, I am aware that from a cosmic/karmic sense we all serve one another—no matter how bizarre that service might look to our time/place self. For example, I know in my bones that one of my lessons is to experience autonomy and that begins with self-love. Although I am aware that I incarnated with a high-frequency love vibration, it took me decades to include myself in my loving outreach.

When I view my life from the perspective that everyone in my family did the best we could, taking into account our individual karma, I realize I am more comfortable forgiving others than myself. I was not the perfect daughter or sister or mother even though I did the best I knew how to at the time. My family was not perfect either, and they did the best they could given who they were.

I believe that we all agreed in advance of being born to be part of a specific soul group. I do not know if we agreed on our specific roles in advance, but I am leaning toward that way of thinking. Part of my soul agreement was broadcasting a higher frequency of love. Looking back, that was an ambitious and a naïve soul agreement, considering my family of origin's resistance to my high beam love frequency. Eventually, I left my family system because I needed to learn how to love myself and to embody Joy. However, I did not give up on love. Instead, I created relationships and communities where everyone was honored, and love blessed each one of us.

Engaging with my Edge-Walking Story challenged me to wonder how my heart touches the world. All Wisdom traditions teach that the heart is the seat of emotion, wisdom, compassion, and love. I am also aware that the journey from head to heart is less than six inches! And I also know from experience that God speaks to me in the silence of my high heart, located midway between the human heart and throat, and is the portal to loving, forgiving, and extending compassion.

Moving beyond Personal Story into Edge-Walking Story called me to be aware of the fears of my heart and to surrender anyway. I learned that my sense of control was grounded in my need to know. I prided myself in being adept at using words to comfort myself and to appear knowledgeable and convince others and myself that I was in control. However, words dissolved during the Edge-Walking apprenticeship. Also, I was daily challenged to admit, "I just don't know, and I want to know."

November 18, 2015
My guides added:
Think of the open-heart as the heart-mind and your challenge becomes how to engage your heart-mind. Yes, aligning with a lighter frequency takes awareness and intention.

When I move beyond problem-solving and Personal Story, I remember how to hold space with a wide-open heart. That is one of the gifts I have reclaimed many times. A friend emailed me and said that the pain he was enduring made him feel suicidal. He was alone and possibly dying. We were continents away from one another. Other than holding space for him to connect with his inner truth, I felt I had nothing to offer.

A psychic had promised him that he would die this lifetime as an enlightened being, and there would be no pain—only light. Since he chose to believe her, he was devastated when pain shattered his dying time. Then he became angry. Depression followed. If this reminds you of the pull of Personal Story, you are right.

As I silently held space for him, guidance came through. He was advised to pause and to remember when he had experienced unconditional love this lifetime. Without a pause, he said, "Yes, with my first wife and later a guru and still later with another woman."

Remembering love was his way through suffering, pain, and the quick-sand of Personal Story.

My guides continued to gift me with their spiritual perspective.

May 6, 2017

Trust how much nourishment others get from being around you.

You hold space for people and offer love, hope, and inspiration.

Love also creates room for intuition. Synchronicity, which I sense is connected to the heart of intuition, continued to call me forward and caused me to wonder if synchronicity is another calling card for Joy. Here's why:

December 14, 2017

Frequency is where it is! This afternoon as I walked on the beach, I focused on my friend, Chuck Kearns. Joan Chadbourne, an evolutionary buddy, brought Chuck into my soul family. We became evolutionary buddies over time and his guides channeled that he needed to integrate faith and human love in order to create an easy dying time.

Chuck left his physical body behind the day before and I wanted to check on him. So I opened my heart and announced that I was ready to receive a message from him in case he was free and ready to connect energetically.

No sooner had I issued my invitation than I saw a long column of white light about six feet in front of me that had not been visible before I set my intention. I was startled and took a few steps back, afraid of the consequences if I walked closer. I reminded myself to breathe and then coached myself to walk toward the light. Gently, one small step at a time.

When I was within one foot of the light column, I heard the word "lucidity" in my mind. No more information or awareness came through and yet I intuited that the word was somehow connected to Chuck.

The column of light blinked as I moved around it. I kept looking up and the light column extended as far as I could see. The first three times that it blinked, I questioned if I might be hallucinating and then I decided it was time to make an appointment with my eye doctor. Then the column of light blinked again. That's when I remembered that Chuck and I had agreed on a wink as a sign that he had successfully bridged dimensions.

"Thank you, Chuck," I yelled, "God speed."

I felt the Joy of connecting with Chuck's soul and marveled at his ability to manifest a sign so early after his arrival in his afterlife.

♥ ♥ ♥

BOUNCING BACK STORIES

Taking up residence in Edge-Walking Story did not exempt me from being triggered and feeling like a victim of my Personal Story. Familiar hard-wired themes and patterns that have the power and the history to bounce me back into Personal Story persisted. Being aware of my core vulnerabilities was important.

The following Bouncing Story continued to challenge my core identity as well as my well-established core beliefs. Three days after cataract surgery on my second eye, I awoke in the middle of the night scared and begging for someone to hold me. I felt like I had regressed to being a five-year-old child and I wanted a strong man to protect me. None of it made sense to my rational mind because the surgery was over.

I was surprised that I connected comfort and safety to a man. I knew from experience I could count on my women friends for comfort if I reached out to them; however, in my vulnerability, I wanted a warrior and I associated warriors with men.

I ran through a list of men friends who I sensed might be comfortable being in a warrior role. Several lived far away. Then I thought of my two closest men friends who lived nearby. I looked at the clock and it was 2:59 AM.

"Too early to call," I rationalized to myself. Then I put two more blankets on my bed, cried, and eventually went back to sleep. However, the "feeling memory" of being young and vulnerable stalked me throughout most of the next day. I felt compelled to figure out my part in the story like someone who is grieving feels compelled to tell their story over and over again.

The next day I remembered that I have curled up and comforted many women and a few men. Some when they were dying; others when they were in extreme emotional or physical pain. I do know how to hold space for others. Each time I remembered how privileged I felt to be part of the healing circle.

The following day I played bridge with both of the men whom I had considered calling in the middle of the night. The bottom line for me was that I wanted to know who and what I could count on from members of my spiritual family. I took a big breath and began. They each listened politely. Then silence. I felt like a child again and struggled to stay present.

One asked, "All you wanted was comfort, right?"

"Right," I replied. "Remember I felt like I was five years old and terrified and I needed someone to hold me."

As if reading his mind, I reassured him, "Sex was not on my mind."

Then I was shocked that my request was sexualized.

More silence. Even when I reassured them that I did not plan to regress again, nobody said a word, including my two women friends who sat at the table. I forced myself to look into the eyes of my two male friends and realized that if either one of them had called me and asked me to comfort or protect them in the middle of the night, I would have been there.

"What stopped you from calling?" my other friend asked respectfully. Without thinking I replied, "Good girls do not call men to come over in the middle of the night to protect and comfort them."

I was gob smacked by the intensity of my judgment. Then I was aware that I was withdrawing, like a cat licking her wounds, and I did not want to do that. I was not a Jezebel. I needed a protector.

Silence deepened. Everyone lowered their eyes. I felt alone and scared because my friends' responses felt so much like my own family where I was punished or mocked for having emotional needs. What I most wanted to hear was, "You could have counted on me," or "Call me if you need support—no matter what the time."

Then the conversation ended. I wanted more. But that did not happen. I reminded myself to breathe so I would not disappear into shame. Energetically and emotionally, I distanced myself. Shame almost claimed me until I reminded myself that I was an adult, and I was capable of caring for myself. Then we resumed our card game as if I had never spoken.

I persisted in trying to see my way clearly through this replay of my family story. I talked to Meghan Don, my spiritual mentor, about the double vulnerability that I was carrying in my heart. She was not surprised that the men had retreated to silence. Then she said, "Women are more accustomed to holding one another, and men, no matter how spiritually evolved they might be, associate holding a woman with sex."

I felt driven to know whom I could count on for comfort. I re-told my story to a couple of my women friends, attempting to arrive at an understanding. One friend explained how my request for comfort without sex might have thrown my two male friends into a vulnerable and unknown place. I appreciated the feedback.

When my evolutionary buddy, Robert Powers, heard my story from his wife, Ellen, another evolutionary buddy, he said that he would have no problem being in the protector role and holding me. He speculated that the elusive past life where I was blinded that had popped up in response to the cataract surgery might have happened when I was a little girl. Later I learned that I had my tonsils out when I was five years old. I have no conscious memory of that event except stories that both my mother and grandmother told me of how much I enjoyed eating ice cream after the surgery. However, I now acknowledge that my body held the memory.

Robert said compassionately, "Rosie, there is a bed upstairs and we can go lie down now and I will comfort you." I appreciated his offer, but I no longer felt in need of comfort.

That brings me back to the enduring family story of being an infant and crying and screaming because I was hungry. Doctor Spock did not believe in feeding when hungry—only on a schedule. Both my grandmother and my mother told me stories of how they put me in the bedroom and closed the door. I cried and cried until I cried myself to sleep. Whew! There it is again. Abandonment.

A few months later when I told Squidge about feeling vulnerable after my eye surgery, she was silent and her eyes sparkled. Then she said, "Whether or not a man accepted your invitation, Rosie, your vulnerability arose from your unconscious and asked acknowledgment from you, and you listened."

Then we talked about the scene in the movie, *The Big Chill*, when one of the women wanted to be a mom. One of her friends volunteered her husband's sperm. He was deeply in love with his wife and yet also respected and cared for their friend and entered into the act with love.

Squidge said, "And that is when the conversation about comfort and love between men and women stopped, Rosie, and you dared to go beyond the conventional by asking your two men friends to comfort you as you engaged in your spiritual transformation work."

Healing happened eventually. I learned that I could be vulnerable and request support. Most of all, I learned how to persist in reaching out for support when I felt traumatized without judging myself as being defective. I also learned that I could count on myself in an emergency.

I tend to be an optimist. Maybe that's why I believe in Divine Right Order. That all changed when a distant family member was murdered while she was food shopping. Her death challenged my belief and I struggled to avoid reacting with fear and cynicism that defines Personal Story.

A few weeks after her death, Noah, my teenaged grandson, and I were driving home from a meditation class on a rainy morning. I saw a teenager carrying a large grocery bag walking beside the dirt road. Ordinarily, I would have stopped and offered her a ride. The idea that my kindness might put us in jeopardy never would have entered my mind or heart.

I overrode my fear, rolled the window down, and asked her if she wanted a ride. She was hesitant. I felt sad because we were afraid of one another and that felt wrong. Then she looked more closely at us.

She stammered, "I guess it will be okay. You two look sort of okay."

"You, too," I said and smiled.

When we were one street away from her house, she ordered me to stop, saying, "My mom would not approve of me riding with a stranger."

"Mine, either," I said.

Later I wrote about how my world had changed since Wendy's death. Yet today I chose kindness over fear because I know that fear eclipses Joy.

My most recent example of knowing I was in danger of losing traction with my Edge-Walking Story began when I was feeling anxious and fearful about an upcoming cataract surgery as related in Chapter 1. Then I felt vulnerable and I judged myself as a coward even though I knew that judging and comparing are elements of Personal Story.

Earlier in the week at Friends Meeting, I announced that I was in the middle of a vulnerability crisis and I felt tender and protective of myself. I felt both proud of myself and a little embarrassed for breaking rank with my family's rule of silence by sharing my emotional vulnerability out loud. I was born an empath and felt everything—until I learned I was not safe. As I grew up, I shut down my feelings and tried to ignore my emotional needs to win acceptance and love. Conformity came with a huge price tag.

Most of my friends would describe me as courageous, yet I was anxious about my upcoming cataract eye surgery and then shamed myself for feeling scared. I tried my best to avoid sinking into Personal Story. Cautiously, I shared my concerns with a few close friends. Each person reassured me and shared their success stories about how simple the surgical process was as well as their stunning results. However, my anxiety persisted.

Three days before the surgery, a healing angel visited me and left an energetic fragrant yellow rose behind. I vaguely remember that she reassured me and counseled me about self-compassion. I was clueless about the interconnection of compassion and safety. Then a friend reminded me that the yellow rose is a symbol of Kuan Yin, Goddess of Compassion. No coincidence that I caught whiffs of the rose fragrance when I swam, walked the beach, or showered. I felt Joy arising as my evolutionary buddy, Diane Powell, surprised me with a real live yellow rose that she delivered a day before the surgery! Eventually, I committed to try to be more compassionate to myself.

Although I was nervous on the day of the first surgery, I reframed the "pinching" sensation in my left eye during surgery as angel kisses and giggled. That's when the doctor commanded me to be quiet.

The healing angel remained in my energy field until the day after the second successful operation. Moments before she left, she said,

"There is something important that you have not understood." Before I could question her, she continued: "Your consciousness is becoming a landing strip for angels and it is essential that you understand about sacred reciprocity from our perspective."

I giggled and then wondered if angels needed people in radio towers to ensure their safety.

♥ ♥ ♥

CREATIVITY AND JOY

I was surprised when Lynda Marvin thanked me for my "creative courage" for daring to sculpt stone which is less forgiving than oils and clay. I searched for my lineage of creative ancestors. I found none. I moved on to historical women who I might adopt as my creative muses. An image of Hildegard of Bingen, *Mystical Visions,* quickly moved into my heart.

Her mandalas, prayers, music, and herbal remedies are infused with creative courage. Neither music nor art was present in the family I grew up in. I was gifted with an active imagination and caught on early that fantasizing, which I excelled in, was judged as "wasting" in my family. I was the first-born child in our family and college was a mandatory requirement. There was no room for imagination when I was supposed to be busy preparing myself for college. I learned how to excel by memorizing facts and concepts. Creative courage was not encouraged. Writing in my journal helped me to gain more clarity.

October 8, 2014

Creative courage means I risk not knowing or even why.

Creative courage means I persist even when I feel discouraged.

Creative courage means I dare to align more with my eternal soul than my time-place ego.

Creative courage calls upon me to surrender and trust.

Creative courage insists that I embody my Truth.

Creative courage insists that I follow my imaginative inner voice.

Creative courage re-awakens me to Joy.

Creativity is both my longing and my shadow. According to research, one of the deepest, enduring beliefs that interrupts women's creative process is our collective belief that we will rupture or destroy important relationships if we commit ourselves to our unique form of creative self-expression.

Over decades I have sacrificed my own creative expression to serve as a muse for men and friends I loved. Future Pull called upon me to fire myself from being overly generous with my energy to others to feel loved.

August 20, 2014

I carry a freeze-frame of the moment, six years ago when Squidge ordered me to make my rattles thinner because there needed to be more space inside for sound. I had no idea how to begin thinning from the inside out. Who knew that using less—not more—stones, shells, or clay pellets added to the sound? What a perfect metaphor!

Then she suggested that I make a bigger opening because I had perfected the technique of joining two pinch pots together and was ready to move on. When I had completed that task, she advised me to consider making the rattle as one piece, rather than my preferred way of joining two halves. I felt inspired and humbled when she compared my time praying in the kiva to the inside of my rattles.

I recorded my intention in my journal to gain more traction.

December 17, 2015

Boldness and boundaries—I call upon you!

I reclaim my ability to be bold as I set my priorities.

I commit to being creatively generous with myself.

Claiming space to explore my creativity felt revolutionary. Setting boundaries with my time and energy felt like a life skill that I had missed out on learning. In honor of my commitment, I lit a tall white candle and watched as the flame melted away my resistance. The questions that continue to circle me and won't go away include:

Who might I become if I made time and space for creativity, silence, and inspiration?

What will happen to me if I become enchanted with my creative potential?

What will I be asked to surrender?

I have no idea what to expect since I have never surrendered to my creativity, yet I know in my bones that creating regularly is important for my well-being and Joy. In honor of femifesting my creativity, I rented office space. It felt like a huge risk since I was a full-time resident grandmother and doing only a few soul readings a week.

Synchronicity reinforced my commitment to explore my creative self-expression when my favorite online astrologer, Eric Francis, weighed in with his weekly advice: "You must use your intelligence, your creativity, and your charm to make sure that you do what you value and that others value what you do."

Synchronicity visits when I am immersed in the fullness of flow. Then I often re-affirm my delight with the light. Next I check to see who wants to join me rather than focus on who is overwhelmed. What if I allowed myself to believe that enjoyment is an open door to the Infinite where all possibilities co-exist?

Sculpting stone, like writing, is all about perspective. When I meet a stone, I hold it in my hands and look at it from all directions, including turning it upside down. Whenever I spot an edge, I purposefully file it into a smooth curve. If I chip away at the front, I check out the sides and back to get a sense of what needs to happen next. Like when I write, perspective matters.

As I hold the stone and observe, the next gesture comes to me, like writing the next line in a well-crafted poem. Often as I breathe in sync with the stone's emerging form, an idea, a word, or even a sentence bubbles into my consciousness. I repeat it out loud as I caress the stone. Then I reach for a nearby piece of paper and record the words before returning to my stone.

At some point, curiosity takes over and I experiment with what might happen if I file more deeply, chip more purposefully, or chisel more playfully. Unlike clay, I cannot replace a part of the stone once I have chiseled a piece away. I take a breath and lead with boldness. Then I breathe and ground myself by remembering the voice of my college graduate advisor as he challenged me saying, "The less you risk, the more you lose when you win." Risking Joy adds momentum.

Later in the day, I returned to my journal and wrote:

April 19, 2016
I am discovering that I have a lot of creative energy available. I cannot quite believe that the more energy I use, the more energy I have available. This principle seems reverse to the way I believe life to be. Usually, the more I use, the less I have.

FOR THE BEAUTY OF THE EARTH

To move fully into Edge-Walking Stories, I believe that we must create time and space for beauty. I agree with the late John O'Donohue, author of *Anam Cara*, who wrote: "In the experience of beauty, we awaken and surrender in the same act." I challenge myself to participate with beauty daily since beauty only visits; it seldom takes up permanent residency—at least for now.

My commitment to beauty, which spans four decades, is essential for nurturing my Joy. Sometimes I feel a need to create beauty. Sculpting is my favorite medium. Writing and playing with words are other forms of creating beauty for me. Other times I choose to be a beholder of beauty. I behold the starry night sky, slide in freshly falling snow, marvel on a spider's intricate web, delight in an apple tree in blossom, and celebrate laughter in the eyes of my two grandchildren.

My guides added their perspective to beauty.

May 19, 2016

Enjoy beauty with all your senses.

Open your heart wide and be inspired by beauty.

Adore flowers and trees.

Adore yourself.

Adore God.

July 6, 2017

Nature is a soul sanctuary for me. My body responds to the beauty of the outdoors. Oceans and beaches used to fill me up. Lakes now remind me of serene mastery. Beauty and Nature have always felt like twins to me.

The land nurtures me more than most people. During the long, gray winter months in Maine, I grounded myself in the earth. A seven-foot ficus tree occupied a corner of my office. The large green pot was large enough for me to stand in. More than once during an interminably long winter, I removed my shoes and socks and stood in the earth that surrounded the ficus tree. Occasionally a client walked in on me and we laughed. Unfortunately, the container was not large enough for two!

I count on the earth. I receive reverence and give back reverence to Her. The earth is my mother; I am her child. I am her servant; she is my soul. I bow in gratitude and the earth receives my reverence, and together we create a sacred circle of reciprocity, which weaves throughout eternity.

Tenting out for the two summers of 2014 and 2015 was a return to the mother's womb—be it whether her womb is in the earth or in the sky. Being outside alone in the middle of the forest brought me back to my relationship with the Divine

Mother and re-connected me with my evolving Edge-Walking Story. My adventures with the night sky moved me into the vastness and unfathomable wisdom.

As I review my journals, I discovered the following delightful full-bodied entry:

June 24, 2015
Remember waking up at dawn to the coolness of the day.

Remember how the dew on the grass tickled your feet and felt like a cool footbath.

Remember the squeaks in the grass that your bare feet made as you walked home from your tent in the middle of the woods after a deep night's sleep.

Remember the pungent pine tree smells that surrounded you.

Remember the hundreds of flashing lights of the fireflies cavorting in the darkness outside your tent.

Remember the fresh smell of new manure that drifted over to your tent from the field next door.

Remember the magical, rapid descent of cascading falling stars.

Remember the haunting hoots of the owls overhead in the trees at night.

I will no longer compromise my frequency and move away from my power because I make people uncomfortable. My mother was envious of me and the attention people gave me. Eventually, I outgrew the habit of dimming my light to be conditionally loved. Grow or die felt like the only two options. Although I felt like an orphan when I stepped away from my birth family, I also appreciated that I was solely responsible for loving myself.

The bigger question is: Where do I belong? One of the answers showed up the next day in an unusual way. Remember, Future Pull is like a wild card.

A Passamaquoddy medicine man smudged both Noah and me at the Pow Wow. The ritual, the rising smoke, the familiar smell of the sage transported me back through twenty years to when I participated in sweat lodges and smudging ceremonies in Taos, New Mexico. I sobbed.

The elderly Medicine Man looked deeply into my eyes and said, "The sage recognizes you and wonders why you have been away for so long."

I said with passion, "I will return."

Later I reflected in my journal.

I re-learned the power of memory.

I felt my deep longing to visit New Mexico, my soul's home.

I appreciated the power of the smudging ritual to return me to the sacred awareness strand.

And now I will figure out a way to visit Santa Fe and Taos, New Mexico.

December 9, 2016

No question that one of my soul's homes is within the vicinity of Taos, New Mexico. My body recognized the power of the land when I first stepped on the parched earth twenty-five years ago in 1991. The land held me for seven years even though residents warned me that the Sacred Blue Mountain had the power to chew me up and spit me out.

I completed my first book, *Healing Grief–A Mother's Story* in Arroyo Seco in 1996 and co-authored *Harvesting Your Journals* in 1999 with Alison Strickland when I lived in San Cristobal. My daughter, Kelli Lynne, graduated from Chamisa Mesa High School in 1992 and married in Taos. Both of my grandchildren were born in Albuquerque, New Mexico. And that is my present lifetime history without a word about my past life history or a possible future lifetime. I have an intuitive sense that re-visiting the Taos area would move me deeper into my Edge-Walking Story.

In 2017, I returned to my soul's home in Arroyo Salto, New Mexico. My mind was filled with memories and feelings during the twenty-minute ride to the top of El Salto Mountain. I wanted to be calm and empty of thoughts and my inner chatter kept me from being present.

I felt the Pull of the Future and the only hint that I had was to sculpt at the fourth waterfall. Although that made no sense to me because I was not a sculptor when I lived in New Mexico for seven years, I obeyed my intuition.

As soon as I stepped out of my car, I sensed the presence of ancestors and that I wanted to connect more deeply with their energies. Two young Native American men guarded the entrance to the waterfalls. When I explained to them that I had returned to my home in El Salto, they offered to accompany me to the fourth waterfall. Plus, they insisted on carrying my heavy backpack.

The trail to the fourth waterfall was overgrown with shrubs and small trees but my feet remembered the way. I stopped a few times to catch my breath. I was thankful that I was not carrying the fifteen-pound chunk of stone and my tools.

Tears streamed down my face even before I stepped into the cave that housed the fourth waterfall. I remembered winters when the waterfall had frozen and how it reminded me of magic. I also remembered times when I had channeled the Shaman of the Mountain by this waterfall.

The two young men sat at the entrance of the cave in silence. I unwrapped the blue stone, said a silent prayer, and waited. I was surprised that my hands felt hot even though the temperature was about 40 degrees. I felt the welcoming earth grounding me.

I sculpted until my fingers got cold. Time disappeared. Moments before I put my file down, I looked at the oldest young man and sensed that something profound had happened to him while I was filing. His eyes had a faraway look and I wondered to myself if he had popped a peyote button while I sculpted. Then he addressed me for the first time.

"I heard a song while you worked. I have never heard this song before and it came to me like I was guiding a canoe down a river. This has never happened to me before. I am not a singer or a musician and I know the song is for you. May I sing it for you now?"

"Yes, please, but would you sing it in your native language?"

"Do you know Tewa?" he questioned.

"No, but I respond to energy," I said, "and then if you would kindly sing it in English, I would be very happy."

He nodded and sang the first few words in Tewa and I sensed the presence of Mother Mary beside us. When he finished, he said that it was a song about Mary who Native Americans considered the Mother of the Earth and how the colors of her costume changed according to the seasons.

I nodded. Then he surprised himself as he channeled, "She is with you. She sits beside you. She is with you when you sculpt, when you pray, and when you heal." Then he was silent. He shrugged his shoulders and his friend reached out and shook his hand. I got up and walked over and shook his hand, too.

As we walked silently down the mountain, I sensed that his channeled song was another Future Pull call. Mother Mary has been a companion to me three different times in this lifetime. Her Presence and message resounded with love, compassion, and forgiveness. Although I was raised Protestant, my relationship with Mary felt like Mother Mary of the Catholic faith. To expand my relationship with Mary and connect with her as Earth Mother felt like a precious gift.

THE BENEFITS OF GRATITUDE

Gratitude is another bridge to Soul Story. It is a gateway that expands the present and magnifies the future. Recently, I have been aware of how much there is to do to return our country to a place of humanity and kindness. I respond to the dangerous world we live in as a citizen, a Christian, and a woman— although the order fluctuates.

Each day I am aware that I could attend at least a couple of protests, write letters to editors, march, or participate in silent vigils. At a recent Friends Meeting where I engaged with others to build silence, I felt my tiredness, and I remembered someone warning me about compassion fatigue. That's when I realized that I have to be careful of not losing myself in trying to transform our society without also being grateful for what I value. For example, I walked outside yesterday and despite the below-freezing temperature, two dark pink rosebuds had endured the frigid temperatures and were in pre-bloom.

In my experience, the more gratitude that I feel and express, the more possibilities and abundance come into my life. The next Story is an example of how gratitude multiplies and creates its own field of attraction.

On the way out of the restroom at the Philadelphia Airport, I overheard one of the women attendants say to the other, "That is the universal language."

I was curious and boldly interrupted their conversation and asked the woman nearest to me, "What is the universal language?"

"Smiles," she replied and flashed me an enormous smile.

I nodded my head in agreement and returned her smile.

"Do you want to experience another universal language?" I asked with a smile.

They nodded in unison. I reached out and hugged the turbaned woman and then the younger woman. They both high fived me.

As I turned to leave, surrounded by giggles of gratitude, a tall woman about my age walked in and demanded to know what was going on.

"Your laughter is contagious. It pulled me in, and I didn't even need to go to the bathroom."

As if we were one person, the three of us surrounded her and drew her into a group hug. Gratitude became our breath.

Signs of moving out of your Edge-Walking Story and into your Soul Story include: listening and responding to inner guidance and being receptive to grace and Joy.

I learn and re-learn how taking action on guidance creates a feedback loop. By embodying guidance, I communicate to my guides that I value their feedback. Dare I believe that all of us are emboldened as a result of my actions?

My guides visited and blessed me with their spiritual perspectives.

January 20, 2018
Believe that your life experiences matter.
Trust in the impact of your words.
Allow yourself to shine brightly.
Dare to claim time and space for yourself.
Empower, inspire, and love yourself!
Just do it!
Right Here.
Right Now.

A friend challenged me to be bold about being different. I honor that I have moved from seeking approval from others to validating myself. Acknowledging my preciousness, which is my uniqueness, feels like the next step. I am grateful to my evolutionary buddies for provoking me.

As I completed my third re-write on this chapter, Eric Frances, one of my favorite online astrologers wrote:

"As a Pisces, the first place the fire burns is in your imagination. Tune into your seeing power. Above all, focus on healing. Move through the world as if you know exactly what you must do, with the confidence that comes from inner listening. Consider yourself one of those whose role is to protect the world and its people, and as such, stand strong in your own protection."

I sighed and said out loud, "Perfect! Love is my protection."

For me, Joy is one of the bridges between Edge-Walking Story and Soul Story because Joy is grounded in a higher harmony. I agree with David Whyte, author of *Everything Is Waiting For You*, who wrote: "Inside of everyone is a great sound of Joy waiting to be received."

THE MOMENTUM OF LEGACY

According to behavioral epigenetics, the behavior experiences of our ancestors are transferred through DNA. That means that my daughter is manifesting part of my unlived dreams just as I am manifesting part of my mother's unlived dreams. One more step. My granddaughter, Malia, is living part of her mother's unlived dreams! For example, my mother wanted to be a writer. She kept records for the local Historical Society and occasionally wrote an article in their newsletter. She also wanted to travel. I traveled to eight countries and visited thirty-six states! My daughter, Kelli Lynne, who is a respected anesthesiologist, is living out part of my dream to belong to a healing community. I am not sure what part of my daughter's dream that Malia is living out. That is hers to discover.

That is one of the reasons I return to the questions: "What do I want my legacy to be?" "What gets passed on from the life I lived?" That perspective leads me to wonder about how much of who I am as a woman is related to my mother and grandmother? When I imagine myself as a vessel of all the ancestors who came before me, I feel even more motivated to broadcast the essence of love, which is grounded in Joy.

A journal entry moved me, at the time, from Edge-Walking into Soul Story.

August 2016

What did I come here to do? To love, to be inspired, to express myself, to create authentic community, to explore untouched places of my journey, to nurture my creative process, to learn, to celebrate, to gain more awareness, to ground future self, to create a balance between solitude and interaction, to dare to shine my light even brighter, to enjoy intimacy, to establish a deep connection with my Soul by embodying Joy and compassion.

SUGGESTIONS FOR MOVING BEYOND
EDGE-WALKING STORIES
Harvested From My Journals

Enjoy breaking rank with limited thinking and beliefs.

Love yourself first and others second.

Cultivate courage to step into the unknown future.

Nurture your unique creative self-expression.

Treat someone to a drive-by blessing.

Know wonder.

Align with your evolving inner truth.

Cultivate your capacity to be in a friendly relationship with the unknown.

Keep a gratitude journal.

Dare to be weird.

Self reflect.

CLIFF NOTES TO SELF: EDGE-WALKING STORY

Trust knowing through feeling.

Remember to be compassionate to yourself to avoid resentment.

Cultivate the ability to hold your value no matter what happens.

Wherever you put your attention is where you put your power.

The capacity to let go is an indication of how free you are.

Honoring inner and outer rhythm is the secret to balance and belonging.

Transformation requires experience, contemplation, and action.

Write about whatever arises from your heart, gut, or soul.

REFLECTIVE QUESTIONS FOR EDGE-WALKING

Where do you go in your body to resource your self-esteem?

What are the courageous conversations you need to have with yourself?

What is your relationship to suffering and vulnerability?

How do you try to belong to the world?

What is your capacity for inner experiences?

In what ways does your imagination speak to you?

What is your relationship with the unknown?

What do you yearn to awaken and ignite within yourself

QUOTATIONS FOR EDGE-WALKING STORY

"Surround yourself with people who are up to good things."
~AMY AHLERS

"Beauty is the explosion of energy perfectly contained."
~RICHARD HOLMES

"Attention is the beginning of devotion."
~MARY OLIVER

"When Joy is a habit, love is a reflex."
~BOB GOFF

"The more we grow in personal power, the more strongly
our state of being impacts those around us."
~STARHAWK

"Give the fullest attention to whatever the moment presents."
~ECKHART TOLLE

"Evolution is the result of self-transcendence. We reach out
beyond the boundaries of who we were and discover
entirely new ways of being."
~ERICH JANTSCH

"We shall not cease from exploration. And the end
of all exploring will be to arrive where we started
and know the place for the first time."
~T.S. ELLIOT

"Give God the benefit of believing that Spirit is leading you.
Accept the anxiety of feeling yourself in suspense and incomplete."
~PIERRE TEILHARD DE CHARDIN

NOTES TO SELF

CHAPTER 3

Soul Story

*"Whatever brings you the most joy
is your prophetic path."*

~Mirabai Starr

DYNAMICS OF SOUL STORY

Soul Story is the place of heart, empowerment, healing, and Joyful service. To get to Soul Story, I first had to free myself from being dominated by my Personal Story or living in my Edge-Walking Story. That required me to return to my needs, my truth, my passion, and my soul purpose—again and again and again!

We are always transforming from being personally centered (caught in personal history and reactions) to becoming more Theo-centered (serving as a channel for universal energy.) As humans, we think we know how life is supposed to look and how problems should be solved, and we forget that our soul offers perspective and freedom. I challenged myself by asking: "What is the spiritual point of view?" Then I reflected on whether my choice supported Soul Story and life lessons or Personal Story and ego. The next question that arose naturally was: "What is the Joy potential?"

Think of transformation as liberation from playing too small. When I make choices that are aligned with my ego, I separate myself from the sacred strand of my life. Awakening is the gradual yielding of the ego to the soul's agenda. As I expanded my consciousness by shifting beyond limiting patterns, my ego lost power.

Integrity and sovereignty are the foundations of Soul Story. Daring to be present in Soul Story means speaking my truth even if I do not know the whole truth and trusting the future to be a place of revelation rather than fear. Full-faith is required along with discipline and balance.

November 16, 2016

I am intentionally stepping into my authentic truth, and I am challenging every belief that does not resonate with my truth.
I am learning that Truth is irresistible to my soul. Besides, Truth arouses my Joy.

Taking up residency in Soul Story required ongoing awareness, courage, and intention. Along the way, I broke rank with limited beliefs and outdated reactions that did not resonate with flourishing. In the process, I re-trained my subconscious mind. When I activated my intention, I was free to inquire about the Joy potential before I made a decision.

When I am present with the frequencies of Future Pull, I co-exist within the realm of all possibilities. Potential is aroused—including Joy. In a way that I have no words to describe, my gifts femifest more directly and abundantly.

Each time I made an evolutionary choice, I aligned with Future Self. When I befriended Future Self, I became a magnet for Future Pull. When I surrendered to the expansiveness and freedom inherent within Future Pull, I knew from experience that I would be challenged to reclaim aspects of myself that resided within my Future Self.

I don't always know what is in the Highest Good. I do differentiate between feeling good and experiencing the Highest Good. I am aware that the Highest Good may not always feel comfortable because often it means that I have left my comfort zone. For instance, when the energies of Future Pull invited me to Camp Etna, a Spiritualist Camp in Etna, Maine, I had no idea what was being asked of me, and I knew in my bones that following through on the guidance was for my Highest Good.

After three summers of living at Camp Etna, I understand that it was the land that called me. As far out as it might sound, I remembered being a protector of the land when I resided in Spirit. Equally true, I believe my evolutionary buddies, Diane Jackman Skolfield and Don Skolfield were also stewards of the land when they lived in Spirit and we continue to pray for the soul of the land this lifetime.

When the frequency of Future Pull became familiar, I no longer had to connect the dots by returning to my journals—I recognized the frequency of Future Pull as it was happening!

As I set my intention to take up residency in my Soul Story, I knew in advance that I would be challenged to break rank again and again. Also, I sensed that healing my personal shadow and releasing projections were part of the curriculum for embracing my authentic self. Then I discovered this quotation by Andrew Harvey, *The Essential Mystic*, that I recorded in my journal in 2015 and that continues to call me: "Consciousness beyond ego is Authentic Self."

My guides visited and channeled:

Spirit suffers without creative inspiration.

Any polarity is in your mind.

Be grateful.

Be humorous.

Establish a connection with Inspirited Ones.

Overall, be mindful.

Along the journey, I appreciated that perception is dependent on our consciousness and our consciousness is a reflection of our energetic frequency. Consciousness is frequency! Every choice has a range of frequencies and my perception is based on my present frequency. As I consciously make choices that expand my frequency, I attract finer and lighter frequencies. Intuition, synchronicity, creativity, and healing sprout from lighter frequencies.

Then I challenged myself to substitute love for judgment and vowed to make the most loving response that I could make instead of blaming, shaming, and closing my heart.

For sure, the ego has a distinct frequency and the soul resonates with a lighter frequency. The self has a frequency. Relationships have a frequency. Death has a frequency. Even Future Pull has a frequency. I have enjoyed the rare experience of vibrating at the frequency of light, where nothing denser can affix itself to me unless it is my karma. Transitions offer a range of frequencies.

This transformational process challenged both my perceptions and projections. Taking back each one of my projections required courage and stamina. If we are not aware of our limiting beliefs or past life overlays, we are at risk of bouncing back into Personal Story. This awakening process is not for sissies.

Being intentionally committed to my Soul Story created a shift in my consciousness that resulted in new ways of thinking and behaving. During this deeply personal transformational process, I developed new ways of relating that were consistent with my emerging Truth. Coherence became a value.

The transformation from Edge-Walking Story to Soul Story involves:

Shifting from needing to know to surrendering.
Shifting from over-giving to holding space.
Shifting from yearning to belonging to being authentic.

Shifting from doing life alone to co-creating.
Shifting from being okay to being Joyful.

Our culture has little patience for not knowing and even less tolerance for Joy. Radical honesty and courage to move into the unknown future with no guarantees are markers for living Soul Story. Equally true, we need to learn to tolerate being comfortable with the unknown—holding it all and waiting and being curious about what will arise.

There is a depth to not knowing and waiting for the unknown future to reveal itself because we are in a different relationship with time when we realize we are eternal.

Entering the yet unknown future required me to take the first step and then another step. When I made a binding commitment to live within my Soul Story, my journey became a love story.

Since I published *Living Future Pull* in 2017, I became a collector of Future Pull stories. People often sought me out to tell me how Future Pull had impacted their lives.

Recently, a workshop participant treated me to her story about Future Pull. She decided to look for another house to buy last fall because she was ready to move closer to Nature. One day she spotted the perfect lot. The owner was on-site and they talked. With no guarantees that her house would sell and the unhappy memory of having it on the market two years before when nothing happened, she listened to the prompting of Future Pull and took a six-month lease on the property.

Then she put her house up for sale. It sold in two weeks to an extended family with the daughter almost due with twins.

"Everyone on the chain profited," she commented with Joy, "and everyone is happy. I send out thanks every morning when I drive by my old home and notice new flower beds and also a couple of new trees."

Most of my friends do not know that I interrupt myself several times a day to inquire: "What am I being asked to do or be right now?" Then I take action on the guidance.

For me, the ongoing question is: "What am I shaping my life around?" The challenge is being aware of my vulnerability without freaking out or closing my heart.

How do I support myself and others to dare to reside in a place of possibility? I am acutely aware that reflection is one way we gain awareness and that requires claiming and holding space for ourselves. I am grateful for the questions that command my attention.

LOVE'S POWER

Love propelled me to move deeper into my evolving Soul Story. The power of love empowers the lesser ego self to discover the greater soul self. Growing in love became a guiding principle. I have learned about love from loving and also attracting shadow wisdom teachers who taught me about love in the reverse. Sometimes I felt like an emotional archeologist digging up ancient and limited family beliefs to break rank with my Personal Story and to embrace my Soul Story.

August 18, 2013

I know that self-love grounds the merging process. We cannot fully or respectfully merge with another until we have accepted and loved ourselves. Armoring, fierce independence, isolation, shutting down, shame, and depression are the opposites of merging.

Choosing to take up residence in Soul Story demands that I choose myself and who, how, and when to love each day. I came in knowing that Love is the expression of God's Presence. Part of my soul purpose is to love: to love others, the earth, and myself and to expand my love and its multiple expressions. I block a potential miracle each time I withdraw from loving or love itself. Being with love means no walls anywhere, anytime, and any dimension of consciousness.

Love breaks us open and awakens us to a larger spiritual context. Embodying love is a sign of spiritual mastery. As I took action on what Future Pull offered to me and asked from me, more was revealed. My trust and faith grew during the process. Gradually, I learned to be more tolerant of my impatience.

My guides offered their spiritual perspective:

Act with all of your heart and let go of results.

The heart knows no polarity or separation.

The heart knows only love.

Practice love until you become love.

When I sit with people who are dying, many reflect on the question, "How much and how well did I love?" Love is the cosmic glue that connects dimensions.

Understanding love and living love are different. I remember decades ago when Susan Holton, Michael Daniels, and I designed and taught a course called "Androgyny" at the Creative Problem Solving Institute's annual weeklong conference, NYU, Buffalo, New York. We each believed that the truth of love was aligned with feminine consciousness while the love of truth was aligned with masculine consciousness and the challenge was to integrate the polarities.

An essential theme of my Soul Story included convincing myself that I am much more than enough and that I am fully supported by my inner resources and that includes guides and teachers.

Requesting guidance put me at risk of having to let go of what I used to believe, as I challenged myself to discover ways to be comfortable with uncertainty. For example, when I slow myself down and ask, "What is the most evolutionary way I can express love right now?" that's when I feel like I am playing a round of Truth or Dare with the universe. The response is always bigger than I could imagine.

My guides added their perspective:

Affirm the frequency of Future Pull as one of your most precious resources.

Remaining in my open-heart despite conflict is new for me. Trusting that I can maintain boundaries when my heart is open is also new. I acknowledge that when I shut down and close off my heart, I move further away from my authentic self and the possibilities that live within Future Pull. So, I choose to be vulnerable and keep my heart and imagination open to beauty, mystery, and grace. Furthermore, I choose what I bless with my energy.

I memorized the following poem and it has hung on my bathroom mirror for years:

It was not about getting or giving love.
It was about breathing love,
Living love,
Becoming love.
  ~Terri St. Cloud

The challenge is how to show up in loving and useful ways that honors others, the journey, and ourselves. For me, owning my sovereignty required a radical shift from seeing power as outside of myself to seeing power as sourced internally within relationships that included:

my relationship to myself,

my relationship with others,

my relationship with my soul,

my relationship with universal intelligence.

When I adopted a witness perspective, I became available for infinite possibilities.

September 1, 2019
Angel:
Each time you align with your spiritual blueprint (Soul Story),
you vibrate to the frequency of Joy.

Not only are you blessed, but you also bestow blessings on others.

Think of the process as overflow rather than exchange.

Continue to indwell with your Soul Story by announcing
your intention.

Remember to invite those who reside in Spirit to add our
impressions to yours.

Cosmic interdependence amplifies your frequency and expands
and deepens your alignment to multi-dimensional consciousness.
You are stepping into a grand, evolutionary design, Dear One.

THE FREQUENCY OF JOY

My intention to grow into my authentic self propelled me into connecting with the transformative energies of Joy. As I age, I appreciate the connection between Joy and truth. The more authentic I become, the more Joy I experience. Since I began to write about Joy, I have experienced Joy encounters daily. I wonder if it is possible to become a Joy magnet.

Grounding myself in my Soul Story amplifies my capacity for experiencing and expressing Joy. This sacred process of choosing Joy involves opening, receiving, surrendering, and being present for the intimacy of the human heart. Looking back, I do not remember anyone inviting me to make decisions based on the Joy potential. I want my words and actions to increase Joy in the world. Danaan Parry, *Warriors of the Heart*, speculated that people run away from moments of Joy because they are moments of great intensity. Daring to risk Joy is the soul growth place for me right now. I sense that Joy is intimately connected to Preciousness.

Following along with that premise, my soul buddy, Penny Moulis, and I finally saw *A Wrinkle In Time* in an almost empty theatre. I don't remember when I read Madeleine L'Engle's book the first time. I do know that I read it to my grandchildren many times.

One of the themes that touched me deeply was that Meg had to embrace her Preciousness to repel Evil. I had forgotten that one of the fairies gave her the gift of her faults so she did not fall into shame as she battled against Evil. Another fairy said, "My love is always with you,"—not, I love you. That is an important distinction. I was glad the pre-pubescent romance was not sealed with a kiss.

Joy is also a catalyst for deep spiritual awakening and fulfillment. My Joy is connected to my passion. Affirmations that I use to magnetize Joy are:

I am Joyful.

I abide with Joy.

Originally, I asked myself "What Joy is being created from my service?" until I re-framed my original question to read, "What service is being created by my Joy?"

For me, Joy is one octave above happiness. My matriarchal lineage was not happy. Being happy breaks rank in my family. When my grandchildren, Malia and Noah, were in elementary school, I taught them that choosing happiness was a daily choice. At supper, we all shared the happy moments of our day. Slowly, they began to catch on that happiness was a moment-to-moment choice. I embrace happiness as a blessing.

In the movie, *Princess Ka'iulani,* the young heiress to the throne of Hawaii is taken away to a boarding school in England. She pours out a collection of seashells from a velvet bag and examines each one. She tells her companion that they're "Ola" shells. Ola means "life" in Hawaiian.

"You collect them, then attach memories to each one so you don't ever forget. This one's for a day I spent at the ocean with my mother and Aunt Lydia. This one's when my mother died."

"And the other shells?" her friend asks.

"They don't have memories yet—they are the future."

After I read this story, I began to pick up stones. I have over one hundred Joy stones and a supply of blank rocks for future Joy.

One of the gifts of being a dedicated journal keeper is that I can track myself. When I visited Bali, Indonesia more than two decades ago in the '90s, I participated in a healing ritual and claimed Joy and Compassion as my God sparks.

I was in a committed relationship with a man and I did not feel safe expressing either Joy or compassion. Fortunately, I left the relationship and I re-learned that being compassionate toward myself, especially amid transitions, was the healthy alternative. Otherwise, I risked being swallowed up with resentment which ensures that I will regress to Personal Story. One of the wisdom threads that I retrieved during this experience was that if it is surprising in a positive way, it is usually aligned with God.

A funny thing about Joy—I often encountered it when I was too busy having fun without it. That seems like a paradox because Joy is grounded in being present. When I experience Joy as the intoxicating feeling of becoming, I feel I'm home. However, the persistent question remained: "Is it possible to become a midwife to Joy?"

February 4, 2019
Joy uplifts! How much Joy will I allow myself? What are the upper limits of Joy for me? Sending flowers to congratulate my soul buddy, Ellen Powers, was filled with Joy. Her excitement upon receiving the bouquet was worth the cost

of at least ten bouquets! Turns out that it was the 114th anniversary of her father's birth. She was "over the moon" with the flowers and her reaction inspired me to send a bouquet to someone each month. Last month I surprised my Granddaughter, Malia, with an unexpected bouquet for being accepted into college.

Experiencing life as a constant dynamic between feelings, thoughts, and choices aligns me to Soul Story. Living without attachment or judgment is a touchstone of Soul Story. As I grounded myself in my body, I became more comfortable waiting to see what arises. That's when my decades old Mindfulness practice came into play because it is the art of being aware from moment to moment. I challenged myself to find the moment or the place where mind, breath, and body are all one. When all three aspects merge, I am home.

I need to remember to ask: "Will this opportunity improve on my silence or my Joy?" Then I need to step back and take a few breaths. Being detached means that nothing in the world has power over me because I do not assume anything about anybody.

THE GIFTS OF ANGELS

My first encounter with an angel happened in 1993 at Findhorn, the international spiritual community outside of Forres, Scotland. I was sitting in a small, darkened meditation room dug out of the earth. Suddenly I felt light moving inside my head and opened my eyes to search around the earth womb for the source of the light. Then I was aware of a champagne bubble sensation in my head. I did not feel light headed, but rather sparkling light was moving inside my head. The sensation lasted for four days and I wondered if I was in danger of having a stroke.

Someone suggested that I make an appointment to meet with Eileen Caddy, the co-founder of Findhorn and author of *Opening Doors Within*. After I drank two cups of the raspberry-mint tea from fruit harvested in Findhorn's garden, Eileen reached over and held my hands. Although she was silent I sensed she was reading my energy. I sighed and relaxed a bit. As I tracked the effervescent energy moving around in my head, it expanded. I had no idea how my head could hold so much light. I explained my symptoms to Eileen and she said calmly, "Trust that the Findhorn angel knows how best to gain your attention in preparation for you to channel. The angel channels for the good of the community and we will be celebrating the anniversary of Findhorn in a couple of days. I am grateful and very excited that she will give us a message through you at the annual celebration in the community Hall."

I stammered, "But I have never channeled an angel before."

Then I asked, "How many people do you expect will be at the party?"

"Well, the whole community and also many people from the nearby town of Forres. Perhaps upwards of five hundred people."

I felt like fainting.

Eileen continued, "You will be fine, dear. In fact, I predict that you will enjoy the channeling experience. The Findhorn angel always uplifts everyone, and besides, she is charming and funny, too."

Then she sensed my panic and offered to sit next to me and hold my hands, if necessary. She got up and poured more tea and described some of her experiences with the Angel of Findhorn as naturally as if she were talking about washing dishes.

The night of the anniversary party, Eileen introduced me to the group of about four hundred people. Then she pulled up a chair next to mine and adjusted the microphone. I grabbed her hand and squeezed too tightly.

I came close to hyperventilating and my vision blurred. Then I remembered to breathe and managed to outdistance performance anxiety. I was relieved when I felt a tickling sensation in my heart and raspiness in my throat. Words followed about the importance of the four R's: Responsibility, Roles, Rules, and Rituals.

When the words stopped, I opened my eyes. I took a few breaths until I felt like I was the only occupant in my body. The group stood up and applauded. Eileen leaned over and hugged me and we both cried.

In 2008, when I was sixty-four, Big Angel joined my consciousness. I sensed the angel's energetic presence for a few months before I received a message. I was conducting a "Presencing" workshop at Leapin' Lizards, my favorite metaphysical bookstore in Portland, Maine.

Big Angel announced "his" presence and asked for permission to teach the group how to align with their Future Selves. None of the participants suspected that an angel was channeling the session because he had merged into my heart. I looked and sounded normal. Yet I was in awe of the simple yet profound process that he facilitated. I felt pregnant with the Divine.

During the group, he channeled:

BIG ANGEL: *I am an inter-dimensional, which means I serve many dimensions.*

My assignment is to remind you of the Truth and Beauty that lives within each of you.

Many are the ways to attract us: silence, intention, beauty, fragrance, curiosity about past and future lifetimes, reading the words of prophets and mystics, creative acts, love, writing without thought, joy, kindness, living from your heart, and prayers.

Allowing yourself to believe that everything is possible is another way to connect with the angelic realm.

My mission is to help you remember all of who you are.

July 8, 2008

My priorities are changing. I desire to be quieter and in communication with Big Angel. When I choose to communicate, I surprise myself by being outrageously unself-conscious and saying whatever I am hearing in my heart.

The channeling from Big Angel is simple:

Just do it!

Affirm and trust that more will be revealed as you take action.

One small step is all that is necessary, at first.

Then more is revealed, and more is demanded.

Then he told me that energetic portals had opened to welcome angels that belonged to deep space. Their role is to support the individual acceleration of DNA—both biological and spiritual.

Remember that I wrote that Future Pull is a wild card and that often pain pushes until Future Pulls? I decided to visit Mountain Light Sanctuary (Retreat Center) and my soul buddy, Michael Lightweaver, outside Asheville, North Carolina, to relax after sending *Soul Befriending* off to the printers. After five days of savoring silence, beauty, and heart centered conversations, I drove to a hotel near the airport for an early morning flight home to Maine.

April 28, 2015

I am waiting for the hotel elevator with my friend, Nancy Carlson. The door opens and two men, deep in conversation, got out. I put my hands out in front of me to stop the first man from colliding with me. I thought I was safe when the second man stepped in back of me, and the next thing I knew I hit the stone floor hard. My glasses flew off my head and I bit through my lower lip. I could not move for several minutes and I feared I was paralyzed.

The men disappeared fast. Nancy looked back when she heard me crash to the floor. She was too stunned to reach down and help me. Somehow, I managed to get myself off the floor, but I could not control my shaking body.

Initially, I believed that the men were aligned with the forces of darkness. No longer because, in retrospect, I realized that the event forced me to claim my healing ability. I refused to talk about the painful incident, as Nancy suggested, because I did not wish to re-enter the trauma. Instead, I swallowed two Tylenol and put myself to bed.

While alone in the bedroom, I tried to download a healing blueprint. No luck. I was in pain and frustrated. Nothing seemed to be working the way I imagined healing worked. That's when I spotted the two angels. I eavesdropped as they talked as if this was the most natural thing to do.

"Are all humans like her?" asked the smaller angel.

The bigger angel did not respond. A few minutes passed with no more conversation.

Then the smaller angel asked the bigger angel, *"When do you think she will remember that she is a healer and put her hands on her back?"*

I waved my hands to get their attention. They disappeared. Although it was painful for me to place my injured left hand in the middle of my back, I did, and felt instant high heat. My spine relaxed and I sighed. I continued to send myself healing until I fell asleep.

A few hours later, while floating at the pool, I unearthed a vow of humility that I had made in a past lifetime. Instantly, I understood how that vow was tied to my reluctance to be more visible as a healer. When I released the vow, I also reclaimed my healing abilities. I am catching on, that once I accept that healing is a Divine right and that I am worthy, I open the door to spontaneous healing.

In my experience, each time that I go to a deeper level of consciousness, healing happens. Then I go to an even deeper level and healing happens again. And then I drop another level deeper into alignment with wholeness.

February 18, 2018
The angels returned a day after my second cataract surgery. Lying in bed a day after my second surgery I realized that I was out of my body listening to angels conversing. Although I occupied the same space-time continuum as they did, I felt far away from them and myself.

I moved closer and realized they were talking about me and I witnessed myself in bed at the same time.

"There is something you haven't grasped and applied," one of the angels said directly to me.

I moaned. "What's that?" I asked.

"We cherish and behold you with the same frequency that you receive us.

We are as delighted with you as you are with us.

We love you.

We resonate with your light and your humor.

We connect to your sensitivity and your vulnerability.

You are precious to us and we behold you with boundless love."

I clapped in response to the message.

*"However, when you fail to receive yourself as precious,
you limit your ability to connect with your heart and us.
The potential for channeling and healing diminishes."*

I exhaled deeply from the bottom of my belly.
"Yes, your essence is radiant."

My ego was on super alert with the light-dimming
question: "Who do you think you are to even think of
claiming Preciousness?"

I have felt loved unconditionally a few times this lifetime,
and yet I sensed that being "received in my preciousness"
went way beyond the moments of unconditional love that
had graced me. As I felt into their frequency, I realized that I
was holding my breath.

"In time you will cherish yourself as much as we cherish you.

*And you will remember that the more you embrace your
Preciousness, the more space you create to receive our guidance.*

*Are you willing to let go of beliefs that separate you from your
Preciousness and to honor your Preciousness as a blessing?"*

I nodded, appreciating that wisdom was offered and
received and I would no doubt get the superhighway lessons
in the next days and weeks.

With one swift motion, I returned to my physical body,
eager to affirm my Preciousness. I felt imbued with sacred
wisdom and I wanted to honor my Preciousness.

I am a creator of rituals. I have created simple rituals to
honor the moon, the seasons, breakthrough events, as well as
recovery from depression.

Instinctively, I decided to re-enact a recapitulation ritual
that I learned from Carlos Castaneda, *The Teaching of Don
Juan*. I lit four long candles and committed to remaining
in the chair by my altar until I was finished. Next, I made a

strong intention to return to my first memory of when my Preciousness was honored or dishonored by others or myself. I allowed the memories to pass through my consciousness and gave gratitude or forgiveness for each memory.

Rituals have their own timing. Seven and one-half hours later, I declared the ritual finished. The next morning the principle of co-arising seduced me into regressing to my Personal Story when I backed into a truck that was parked behind my car in the driveway. The timing was absurd! This was the last day of five years of car payments. Immediately, my punishing ego kicked in and I shamed myself until I recognized that I had strayed universes from my Preciousness. Then I took a few breaths and headed for the beach to walk myself back into my Soul Story.

The greater the transformational edge, the more our ego will push back. I call this the principle of co-arising. Co-arising happens. Welcome it! Think about it as the pull of the past that offers another opportunity to affirm your intention. When I teach, I alert my students to the challenge of co-arising because I want them to avoid getting hijacked by a shame attack. For example, when I affirmed my Preciousness, I almost surrendered to a shame attack. Whatever is not aligned with Preciousness in my consciousness will arise to be transformed. No exceptions!

Unfortunately, the challenges did not end with the car incident. The following day I flew to Florida to attend my Goddaughter's wedding. As I munched on an avocado sandwich, my front tooth fell out. There was no time to consult a dentist because the wedding was the next day. Although I knew that I was not directly responsible for the gap in my smile, I lost contact with my Preciousness again. It was my vanity that was bruised this time, and I retreated from Soul Story until my sense of humor returned and I re-named myself Pirate Woman.

Two weeks later I dropped a recently completed black and green sculpture named Source onto the concrete sidewalk as I attempted to balance my tool bag, sandbags, and the polished stone. I chided myself about the fissure that created a deep uneven scratch along the bottom. Then I realized I had disappeared into my small Personal Story and Preciousness was missing-in-action.

Gradually, I affirmed Preciousness because that was the opposite of judging. The first time I said out loud, "I am Precious," I felt a slight bit of movement in my body. Then I shook my head because I was aware that it was easier for me to affirm that the sculpture was precious. I persevered and knew I was free of Personal Story when I spontaneously kissed my hand and then kissed the sculpture.

Source now shares a space with Angel of Compassion on my mantle. The meaning I made out of this incident was that I am Precious despite my brokenness. The sculpture is precious despite the crack. I am on the edge of understanding that when I am self-conscious or self-absorbed, which happens, in Personal story, neither Joy nor Grace visits.

Honoring my Preciousness, as do the angels, means that I am gentler with myself. When I am tired, I rest. When I am sad, I cry. When I am grateful, I express appreciation. When I am frustrated, I move on. When I am vulnerable, I reach out.

I re-learned how efficient my guides were and how synchronicity is as natural as my breath when I follow my inner guidance.

I re-discovered that Preciousness and Joy are partners.

I appreciate that breakthroughs offer gifts and ask for something from me in return.

And now I will sparkle.

February 24, 2018

I continued to be amazed by how the holy ones are as filled with delight at connecting with me as I am when I connect with them! How did I miss that connection for almost three-quarters of a century? In what ways would my life have been different if I had remembered that cosmic and human truth at birth?

While I was in between sleep and awake, I understood that love times two equals Joy. All exists in reciprocity. My willingness to honor my preciousness amplifies love, Joy, and healing. I know that in my bones. As the holy ones serve us, we too serve them by allowing ourselves to know that we are treasured by them. Whew! What would our world be like if we all believed we are the beloved of the Beloved?

What I didn't know about the angel visit is how love aligns with Future Pull and Soul Story. I am surprised again and again when I experience myself and others closing ourselves to the irresistible frequency of love. I know another way—love is my way. Being open to love is an evolutionary choice.

February 26, 2018

I surprised myself by saying out loud at a friend's house, "I feel like my consciousness is a landing strip for angels recently." She laughed and said she was not surprised because of the light that I carried. I do not know how the angel infusion happened; however, I am Joyful to serve in this way.

Whenever evolutionary buddy John Hornecker and I meditate, I appreciate how easily we merge. I suggested that we meditate with the intention of receiving information about how to be in alignment with our guides during our three days together.

The moment I closed my eyes, a slim, magnetic silver band was placed over my forehead. The guides channeled that it was a device to empower others to remember cosmic possibilities as a way of uplifting mass consciousness.

Next, I sensed the presence of a radiant angel. She channeled that embodying kindness, cooperation, gratitude, and discovery guaranteed a shift into expanded consciousness. The information seemed practical, and I am excited to live it.

April 7, 2018

ANGEL: *Merging is not the same as co-dependence or enmeshment. Always our perspective is one of interdependence.*

ME: I realize I have expended a lot of energy being independent to override my early training to be co-dependent. Yet the term "interdependence" is like an unknown color to me. How can I open to being more interdependent?

ANGEL: *Allow and be. No need to struggle. Dismiss "doing" gently.*

Interdependence is collaboration.

Improvisation is a close relative to interdependence in your human dimension.

When you are present, you are open and attract more refined energy.

Breathe into the fullness of that energy.

Then allow yourself to relax even more.

Be of an open heart.

INTUITION AND JOY

At a recent conference, several people wanted to hear my thoughts on intuition. They seemed surprised when I said simply, "If you want your intuition to grow, love more."

Then I told them that decades ago I invented a game called Cosmic Catch. I was accustomed to my guides tossing a "blink truth" to me and I caught it. I never knew when the cosmic catch game might happen. I was unaware that I could initiate the process. Until the first time! When I became comfortable tossing an intuitive question in ball form to my guides for answers, I expected a reply and was seldom disappointed. The game was a perfect example of reciprocity in action.

Action is an important part of the feedback loop. Action means I value the information even though I might not understand or appreciate the guidance initially. Putting legs on the guidance by taking an action step gives guides feedback that I am a serious student.

The following journal entry is a perfect example of reciprocity:

May 29, 2018
After a long workout at the local recreation center, my guides ordered me to take a walk on the beach to find a hospice nurse for my friend, June Bro, while I resided in Maine for the next four months. Seldom do my guides command. However, I resisted the beach jaunt because I had already exercised. A few hours later my guides insisted that a beach walk was important. No more information was given. I sighed and fired myself from complaining and resisting because they are hallmarks of Personal Story.

Within five minutes of walking on the deserted beach, I spotted a woman leaning over something on the sand. As I came closer, she picked up a baby sand shark and lowered it back into the ocean. When I thanked her for rescuing the shark, she shook her head and said, "It won't live. I know a death rattle when I hear it. I am a hospice nurse."

I was not ready to announce that we were supposed to meet up. The synchronizers were at work. We continued walking together like old friends and she mentioned that she planned to take time off to write a book about meditation and dying. I commented that writing takes lots of focus and alone time. Then she announced that she was an evidential medium.

I quipped, "Are there any other kinds of mediums except evidential?"

She laughed and I told her I was one, too. Then she said she had tried to gain clarity about an issue from her guides and the answers did not make sense. As if we had been friends forever, she asked me if I would channel for her.

"What's the question?" I asked.

"If you are a credible medium, you would know both the question and the answer," she replied.

I laughed out loud. Touché! I liked this woman who told me her name was Sara!

Then I tuned in, and her guides provided the evidential information that she requested. We high fived one another and continued walking.

Sensing it was time for me to ask her for a favor, I told her how my guides had insisted that I line up a hospice nurse for my friend. Then she told me that not only was June Bro a friend, but that June had counseled her when she was going through a tough time during her divorce. Then she added that June had also taught her daughter piano lessons. The deal was sealed right there on Chic's Beach.

I was surprised when she asked me to walk to her house because she wanted me to see something on her dining room table. I did not have the time to follow her home. Then she said that her guides had chanted the name Rosie so loud in the early morning that she had written my name on a piece of paper and placed it in the center of her dining room table! It was my turn to giggle and throw my arms up to the sky. We hugged and laughed.

The story does not end with our beach walk. The next day when I opened the door into June's apartment, I spotted Sara singing and dancing for June. Not only did she have a great voice but she also moved like a dancer. June was excited that we had found one another. Thank you, guides!

I re-discovered that reciprocity is the cosmic glue for Soul Story.

I felt blessed.

I appreciate how magic doubles when two people listen and follow their intuitive guidance.

And I will continue to be an outrageous magnet for Joy.

Channeling is another example of receptivity, surrender, receiving, and taking action. Since we carry the stardust of the cosmos, we can communicate from that place of awareness and understanding. As if waiting to be called, my guides channeled:

Dare to channel pure Spirit.

November 25, 2009
It is the energy of softness that readies a heart to be light.

Soft focus, soft-touch, soft heart.

To expand even more, you need to embrace softness in all dimensions.

It is lightness of Being that motivates you to rid your consciousness of outdated beliefs to be more present.

A soft focus invites a deeper awareness and a reverence for the process.

Softness is an attribute of your soul.

Be assured that softness is not the same as gullibility.

When I ask, "Why me?" and "Why now?" the answer I receive is *"Because some people need to be reminded of their light, which vibrates to Truth, Spaciousness, and Wisdom."*

I remind myself often that there is no sequence in fifth dimension reality because when I try to use my mind to figure things out, or to reconstruct events, I frustrate myself. Present-day language does not serve fifth-dimensional reality so I have to be content doing the best I can.

I am pondering about the energetic difference between firm, fierce, and gentle strength.

July 17, 2019

Ariel Silver, one of the instructors at IWWG (International Women's Writing Guild) and a songwriter, invited my evolutionary buddy, Alison Strickland, and me to join her after supper as she rehearsed "Mike's Song" for the Opening ceremony. Not only did I want to hear every word, but I also wanted to know every detail of the story behind the 4:09 minutes of the song.

She told us that, after the IWWG conference last July, she visited a Native American museum, and the title of the exhibit was "I know more than I can explain." According to her, that's when she remembered—in precise detail—the story I shared with her about the death of my son, Mike, and how he later channeled through me as an "Inspirited One."

According to Ariel, Mike's song wrote itself, including the line, "Life is composed of losses and gains. I am a veteran of both." When she sang the song to her husband, he cried. Her lyric critique group said nothing needed to be changed. She looked directly into my eyes and said, "Rosie, it was like Mike had channeled through me."

I was blown away that a new friend had created a song about my son who had been dead for more than forty years. For sure, I too know much more than I can explain and yet translating the invisible to the visible is my job and my responsibility. Most of the time it is also my Joy.

August 3, 2019

I treated myself to another morning meditation with Rosy D'Elia, a medium from Montreal with a huge heart. She is masterful—even when life has her by her ankles.

During the meditation, I immediately became a thin, straight arrow of light and zoomed high in the sky. I remembered no other details. When the meditation was over, she asked about our experience. I shared how I felt myself as a straight arrow of light.

Then she surprised me by asking if I had a message for her. Without pausing, I channeled, "Keep wearing the necklace you are wearing."

I thought that was the entire message. However, she looked at me expectantly, and I heard the words, "La Luna" inside my head. As I leaned into the silence, I understood that she needed to rejuvenate herself by visiting with the moon. When I delivered part two of her message, she started to cry and said my message was a confirmation.

Then she returned to me and said that she sensed that I was being inspired because when she looked at me, she experienced my head, face, and throat alive with energy. I intuited the inspiration that Rosy saw around me was somehow connected to the clay angel, which Squidge had given me the day before. When she gave me the porcelain angel, she said, "This angel is dreaming you." Yes, dreaming me! How magical! On closer inspection, I was surprised that the brown angel's body resembled mine!

♥ ♥ ♥

August 25, 2019

I am still unsure about what to do with a psychic reading at Healing Light Church in Etna, Maine, yesterday. The medium approached me and said that her guide was talking to my guide and she had an important message for me. I nodded my head in invitation. She said Jesus wanted to channel a book through me and it would be like no other book I have written.

She continued, "Plus, there were several ascended masters waiting to be received by you, too. And they were all thanking you for your receptivity and your work."

I was relieved when she channeled, "The time was not now, but soon."

Then she cautioned me to be careful during the editing process because the words, which in some cases would seem old fashioned, should not be changed.

"There will be nothing of you in the book," she repeated. "It is all channeled."

Recently I have felt the presence of Holy Ones around me and have not been able to decipher the messages. I have not shared this information with friends because it feels beyond huge to me.

I responded to her message, saying, "And I counted on being finished with writing books."

Yet I know there is a difference between writing and channeling. A deeper surrender appears to be part of my future curriculum.

I noticed that people tended to avoid me at the potluck lunch after the service. Fortunately, I did not take their avoidance personally. I was not the only one in awe.

DREAMS AND AWAKENING

Dreams often carry a spiritual imprint because they open the door to our unconscious and show us where we are in the narrative of our lives. I marvel that when I am ready to wrap my heart and mind around an emerging truth, both my dream life and my ongoing conscious life seem to conspire to alert me that it is time to be receptive to a more awakened consciousness. Claiming the new expanded consciousness is the next step.

January 1, 2011

A dream message woke me up in the middle of the night. I had no memory of the content of the dream. However, the essence of the dream continued to beat in my heart: "Listen to the wild invitation in your heart."

Then I wondered: "What is the dream inside me that wants acknowledgment?"

I challenged myself to be true to the wild invitation in my heart when I agreed to co-lead a workshop for women leaders about Connection and Community with my evolutionary buddy, Lou Ann Daly, *Humans Being*. We are both Pisces women and magic happens when we play or work together. The night before the workshop I had the following dream. Many of the women from the workshop are on a retreat in Africa. We are shopping at an outdoor bazaar, and I am fascinated with the colors, fragrances, and fabrics. Lou Ann looks over at me and says casually, "Rosie did you forget something?" I look down and realize I am naked!

"No problem," she says, as she reaches into her large purse and hands me a long, brown caftan. I slip it on. When I pirouetted in front of her, she said, "It will do." When I spotted myself in a mirror, I saw that my backside was exposed. No matter. Dream ends.

I woke up knowing I was ready to be my wild authentic self at the workshop. During the two-day workshop, I spoke from my heart; cried when touched by beauty, truth, pain, or synchronicity; and modeled how to hold space for the emergent design. Joy was present throughout the two days. No question that the energetic frequency of the Divine Feminine femifested!

February 4, 2011
In this vivid dream, I was speaking as my Future Self. From the perspective of future self, I was in touch with precisely what people needed to wrap their arms around to experience a breakthrough. I understood how to introduce them to the frequency of their future selves whether through an exercise, a conversation, an invitation to play, a ritual, or art.

When I described the dream to a friend, she commented, "It sounds like you are coming out."

I agreed and added, "I feel more like I am coming home." I know that I carry the seeds of Future Pull, even though I lack words to describe what that is.

November 14, 2018
Early Saturday morning before the Bridging Generations Women's Group, I awoke from a vivid dream. I was standing front stage before a loud crowd of people. When I turned to write something on the board, twinkle lights escaped from my fingers. Not words—blinking lights. The room became silent.

People stared at the blinking lights on the whiteboard with big eyes. The dream ended and I woke up at the same time!

Sometime later I remembered that I had included the word "Twinkle" on my vision board. When I told the dream in the group, everyone reacted. All agreed that a blinking light draws more attention than one focused, high beam.

My name for the dream was "Show Up." I am eager to take action in my life and Show Up in reality. I shrug off my ego's attempt to interfere by equating Showing Up with Showing Off.

February 3, 2019
I awoke this morning at five with the phrase "I have an appetite for awareness" stamped on my consciousness.

When I wrap my heart around the dream sequence above, my curiosity joins my awareness.

I re-discovered how my dreams beckon me to embrace my Future Self.

I feel in wonderment.

I appreciate the practical wisdom embedded in my dreams.

And I will be even more welcoming of my dreamtime.

MORE BOUNCING BACK STORIES

A Bounce Story that temporarily moved me out of Soul Story happened during a three-day adventure in New York. Among the memories of majestic music, outrageously beautiful holiday decorations, and overwhelming crowds, I recorded another incident in my journal because it almost catapulted me back into Personal Story.

December 23, 2018

My soul friend, Penny Moulis, and I treated ourselves to
a pre-Christmas weekend in New York City to hear Paul
Winter's Solstice Consort. Our excitement was boundless and
we had front row seats!

After we finished a delicious Italian meal, we walked a hard
two blocks toward the Cathedral of Saint John the Divine. We
both were concerned that we might be lost. As we stood on the
corner of a large intersection, Penny asked a woman walking
toward us for directions. She walked briskly by us without
saying a word. We looked at one another in shock.

Then I motioned to another well-dressed woman coming
toward us. She ignored my request, too. For a second I
wondered if somehow we had both died and resided in a
different dimension where people could neither see nor hear
us. Penny, who is more down to earth than I am, speculated
that perhaps the women thought we were looking for a
handout. I dismissed that idea because we were both dressed
up in our best clothes!

I felt like crying and I was annoyed. I hate feeling lost and
out of control. Besides, people were supposed to be friendly to
out-of-towners! Then I pivoted out of feeling like a victim and
commanded Personal Story to be gone!

Neither one of us spotted the elderly man who approached
us, doffed his hat, and asked, "Are you two ladies lost?"

We both nodded our heads "Yes."

"I thought so," he said and laughed.

"Where are you two ladies headed?"

When we told him that we were looking for The
Cathedral, he pointed to the top of the hill and told us to
turn right at the top and we could not miss it. When I asked
if he was sure because I did not want to trudge up the hill and
be in the wrong place.

He exclaimed, "Honey child, even Ray Charles could see The Cathedral."

We all laughed. Then he wished us Merry Christmas and my hopes in humanity were renewed.

♥ ♥ ♥

I had no idea that when I dedicated my tenth book, *Living Future Pull* (2017), to June Bro that I had stepped into another feed-forward event in my life where an event in the present becomes better understood in the future.

During our four-year friendship, we enjoyed being together whether we were sharing a meal, participating in A Search for God Study Group, interacting during her weekly Chat at A.R.E., watching a movie, meditating, praying, healing with the Glad Helpers Group, or competing against one another in our weekly bridge game. We each welcomed Joy eruptions in our personal lives and when we were together, the Joy doubled. Frequent God gasps (Oh my God) were also familiar expressions.

Fast-forward a few years to 2018: During a March weekend getaway to a condo on the Boardwalk in Virginia Beach, I asked June, my spiritual mentor and friend, if she thought she would have any regrets during her dying time. She was sitting at the table watching the sun go down and sipping a glass of her favorite red wine.

She surprised me with her rapid response. "Yes, dear, my soul will be sad that I never wrote my own book."

She smiled at me and continued sipping her wine. A comfortable silence filled the room. I was struck that HER SOUL would be disappointed.

When I recovered words, I asked, "On a scale of one to ten, how disappointed do you think your soul would be if you did not write your own book?"

"Eleven," she said adamantly.

How perfect everything seemed at that moment. I was a published author of ten books. When I was president of Blessingway Books, I resourced Joy by helping first-time authors shape their stories. Plus, I now owned a publishing company! Best of all, June's book had the potential to create an additional income stream for her.

Also, we had both adopted the ideals of Joy and peace and we both welcomed peace as "Joy resting." Equally true, we had both endured pain and suffering in our lives, and yet we each chose to celebrate the Joy strands amidst heartache.

I imagined June and me co-creating Joy and healing as we worked on her memoir, especially since it was a soul agreement for her. I also took for granted that she would embolden herself as she weaved the strands of her Soul Story together.

The rest of our story points out how the dynamics of Personal Story can take over when role and soul conflict. Joy was mostly missing for both of us while June and I worked on her spiritual memoir, *Coming Home To God*. In retrospect, I wondered why I imagined that cooperating on this project would be easy? Then I smile at my naïve response—"Because June and I loved one another"—as if that truth, all by itself, were a free pass to Joy.

The facts were that June was 98 years old, and her memory resided somewhere else much of the time. Her health declined from week to week. I was 74 years old and I forgot my keys, people's names, and sometimes what I was going to do next. I, too, sometimes surrendered to a mid-day nap.

"Sisyphean struggle" are the words that come to mind when I am honest. I have a hunch that June would agree if she were still alive. Pam, her oldest daughter, was right when she said the book project kept her mother alive. What she didn't know was that I felt like I was her Mom's oxygen.

However, as June's evolutionary buddy, I had agreed to shepherd the making of her memoir. Neither one of us admitted that we started too late for June's full participation. I questioned what is right action when one party is not able to live up to their part of a mutual soul agreement through no fault of their own. What are the karmic implications, if any, if a soul contract is aborted?

Midway through the process, I called my soul buddy, John Hornecker, *Cosmic Insights Into Human Expression*, for his spiritual perspective. He listened to my concerns and then he wondered out loud if Harmon and June Bro's "mutual soul mission" to educate the world about Edgar Cayce had expired since Harmon had been dead for more than twenty years.

Then he asked gently, "Rosalie, would the world be worse off if June's memoir was not published?"

I replied instantly, "That's the wrong question, John. I am convinced that the world would be *better off* if her book is published because she has timeless wisdom threads in her memoir. Edgar Cayce was a catalyst for her to create a more intimate and playful relationship with God, and she dedicated the next seventy-five years of her life to applying his holistic and spiritual principles. However, her true legacy is full-faith living."

One week later, November 12, 2018, at his request, I trance channeled Harmon Bro for June. Besides himself, Gertrude, Gladys, and Marguerite and a man named Cameron were there to help her remember from the place in the middle of her forehead, her third eye. He suggested that June think of her memoir, *Coming Home To God,* as another form of service and inspiration with a bit of education blended in. He spoke of spiritual principles. One of his messages was that there are no veils between dimensions. I knew that to be true, and I trusted that my relationship with June would continue to exist when she dies because our friendship feels eternal. June and I both later agreed that he "outed" her for her humbleness.

The following day I walked in a bit late for June's weekly Chat at Edgar Cayce's A.R.E. June was reading the trance channeling to a large group of people. The regular members complimented me profusely. Most of the people had tears in their eyes. I was embarrassed and felt vulnerable. I didn't know what to do with compliments!

As soon as her session was over, I fled home, pulled the curtains, unplugged my phone, and buried myself under my down comforter! My response was bizarre and I questioned myself out loud shouting, "What is going on here?" "Who is living inside my skin?" I stayed with my emotions until I identified that I had felt exposed.

Most people know that I am intuitive, and several people present had consulted me for soul readings. However, few people knew that I was also a medium who trance channeled. I had kept that part of my life private. Based on my dramatic reaction, I must have endured a traumatic past life experience that centered on being a medium. Why else would I have felt so vulnerable and out of control?

It was time to reframe my beliefs about being a medium or be claimed by Personal Story. Before I went to bed, I made an intention to ask Mother Mary for help in cleaning up any karma associated with being a medium so I could move forward in a new and shiny way. She reminded me to extend love and compassion to myself. Gratitude, too. What a relief to be almost outside of the dynamics of Personal Story and looking forward to healing another core vulnerability.

I learned how my unconscious controls me.

I re-learned how to ask for help.

I felt terrified and stuck outside of time until I understood that an opportunity to heal was stalking me.

And now I will be more visible and confident about being a medium.

On December 3, 2018, I trance channeled Harmon Bro at his request for the second time. He pointed out to June that "It is your turn to be center stage so being demure won't cut it anymore." Then he pointed out to her that her weekly Chat at A.R.E. and her articles in *Venture Inward* magazine were examples of playing on a small stage. Her memoir had the power to impact many more people.

Later that month at my monthly women's potluck supper, I asked June for permission to read stories from her unedited memoir. I thought

I was doing it for her so she would be motivated to work more diligently. However, as I was reading excerpts out loud, I realized I was also doing it for me because I felt bogged down. All of the women were enthusiastic and commented on how her stories flowed. A friend said that she had never heard Edgar Cayce described so personally and she understood more about his spirituality. June glowed with Joy.

I enjoyed watching June experience first-hand how her stories impacted others. She was on the edge of her soul's fulfillment when she allowed herself to believe that her experiences, insights, and examples had touched and ignited the souls of every woman in the room. Before I went to sleep, I smiled to myself as I remembered that in the tree of life there is a feminine branch of strength and sometimes it is called tenacity.

Looking back, my monthly women's potluck gathering felt like a dress rehearsal for June's decision to read from her unedited manuscript at her Bon Voyage party on January 20, 2019. More than sixty of her friends gathered in the meditation room on the third floor of A.R.E. for her last-minute going away celebration. She carried the Joy vibration from the women's gathering and that boosted her confidence as she read story after story. Her Joy was contagious in a positive way. Every one of us cherished her as she read from her almost finished manuscript for the first time. (I had read her stories the first time because she wanted to listen to her voice on paper.)

June was on fire to read more and more excerpts. A friend interrupted and asked June for a prayer. She graciously offered a long prayer and a few times I wondered if she was channeling! Then I mentioned how much June liked to hear prayers and invited anyone in the group to offer prayers for June. What an epiphany!

She celebrated her glory moment at her Bon Voyage party. Her community responded with enthusiasm and signed up for advanced copies of her book! I was proud of her and also caught up in anticipatory grief because I was aware that she was moving to Massachusetts in two days to be with her two daughters and son.

August 20, 2019

June Bro died yesterday at 2:30PM. I was sculpting a green healing heart for her. I knew the exact second that she chose to excarnate. I wondered if she had known all along that I was working on the green healing stone for myself.

Alison, her youngest daughter, called a few minutes after June died and assured me that her passing was peaceful.

For months I had expected that she would surrender earlier and yet accepted her choice. I was comforted when Alison said that June's happiest years after Harmon died were the last two-plus years that she lived in Virginia Beach.

The rest of yesterday seemed to dissolve into nothingness after I got the news about June. When I shared June's death with Meghan, my spiritual mentor, she predicted that June's dying is my birthing. I do not understand. Not yet. The end of her life goes way beyond my understanding.

♥ ♥ ♥

August 29, 2019

Today Karlene Tanner, a medium at Camp Etna, in Etna, Maine, dropped by and casually asked if I had any contact with June since her death. Earlier I had shared that June and I had made a mutual intention to communicate after she died. June figured that if Harmon chose to communicate to me, she would give it a try, also. I told her that I was open to communication, but so far, I had not connected with her.

Karlene said simply, "Rosie she needs music. She can connect if you play Clear Loon music."

I looked puzzled and said that I did not understand.

"It sounds like 'Clear Loon' but the communication was a bit staticky because this was her first contact."

I had put down the green stone loon I was sculpting to listen to Karlene. I swim with two loons daily. Suddenly I laughed loudly and said, "She wants me to play 'Clair de Lune.' That was her favorite song and I have a copy of the CD that she made in 2010 in the cottage."

Then Karlene shared with me that my rented cottage is in the original pine tree forest at Camp Etna where hundreds of healers and spiritualists gathered to heal people every summer during the camp's heyday in the early 1900s. She said that the pine trees were so thick at that time that once you stepped into the forest, you could no longer hear sounds from the road or camp. It was like stepping through dimensions! No wonder I felt so peaceful living at the edge of the healing place.

Later I put batteries in my boom box and loaded June's CD. At 7:30 PM I sprayed myself with bug spray and walked the short distance to the pine forest. I sat down on the healing rock that has been in place since 1891 and sent out gratitude to all the people who had blessed the land with their healing energies.

I felt edgy and excited. Next, I played June's CD. Then I opened my heart to June by remembering cherished times with her. Next, I called out her name three times.

No waiting—she was there as if she had been waiting for me to pick her up to play bridge! I burst into tears. Her energy felt full, loving, and present. I felt her closeness as if no space separated us at all. Harmon was right when he channeled that there are no veils. I took a deep breath and felt how much I had missed connecting with her at a soul level during the seven months she had resided in Massachusetts.

June began to communicate with me. "Look, Rosie dear, I no longer have to poop." I laughed because often when we played our weekly bridge game she would say, "Oh, poopie," when she did not like her hand of cards.

Then she corrected me: "Rosie, I don't have to stoop anymore." That made sense, too, since she had used a cane and wheelchair for months before she died and her posture was compromised.

"Rosie," she communicated excitedly, "Mr. Cayce was right. Celestial music is real. Don't you remember when he described hearing beautiful celestial music as he was dying?"

"June, I wasn't alive when Mr. Cayce died."

"No matter," she replied, as if time did not exist where she resided. "And there are no notes to memorize and blend. No notes, no scales, no practice."

Her exuberance made me giggle. She interrupted my laughter and said more forcefully, "I need you to assist me in getting the word out about dying."

I took a deep breath and assured her that I was listening.

"Rosie," she said with some urgency, "I waited too long to die, and I want to spare others that experience by sharing what I realize now. Are you listening, dear?"

"Yes," I replied, "but I thought our soul work together was finished when your memoir was published."

"So did I, but we were both short-sighted."

"Here's how it was for me. When my health started to fail and hospitals and rehab places became my temporary homes, everyone around me treated me like a patient. The doctors and nurses focused on what was wrong. Test after test told them even more about what was not working. I forgot that I had a light body and a soul. It was like I fell under a spell and slowly amnesia set in. If I had remembered my light body, I would have remembered that I had an exit strategy."

"Rosie, I have talked to others here who did not remember their light bodies either, and each one now believes that it was not necessary to suffer and be burdens. It is important to remind people who are dying, and their families, that they have a choice to remain in their compromised physical bodies or to slip into their light bodies. There are others here who will explain the chemistry of the light body if you agree to sign on."

I raised my hands over my head in surrender and said out loud. "I agree if you agree to do your part."

"You know it," she replied.

Before I could thank her, she had disappeared. Until the next time.

I re-learned that my relationship with June Avis Bro is eternal.

I discovered how cranky I am when I do not feel met.

I re-discovered that when I am clear about my vision, I harmonize with the universe.

I felt every emotion on the keyboard and did my best to keep my heart open.

I regret that I was not more compassionate to June and myself.

I appreciate how neither one of us understood that the birthing of June's memoir was one bead in our evolving story.

And now I will savor our continuing relationship.

To order a copy of *Coming Home to God* by June Avis Bro, visit my website at www.heart-soul-healing.com. All proceeds are donated to the June Bro Scholarship Fund at Atlantic University which is affiliated with Edgar Cayce's A.R.E.

THE HEALING POWER OF BREAKTHROUGHS

What happens after a breakthrough? I experience a breakthrough as a blast from the Infinite. Breakthroughs re-arrange our consciousness. A breakthrough moves me closer to my authentic self. At the same time, it can also create stress because friends and family expect us to act "normal." In my experience, something is offered and something is asked of us.

After a breakthrough, I believe that I have a responsibility to continue to partner with expanded possibilities. If my breakthrough is connected to my creativity, I have a responsibility to continue creating from a consciousness of expanded awareness. If my breakthrough is connected to my thinking, I have a responsibility to live into my expanded thought process. If my breakthrough is connected to healing, I believe I have a responsibility to embrace my epiphany.

July 16, 2017

At the Healing Light Church (in Etna, Maine), the medium of the week asked if she could approach me with a message.

I nodded.

First, she said, "You are a healer."

I said, "Yes," with a bit of hesitation.

She continued, "Do you know the Native American medicine man who resides in your energy?"

"Yes," I replied. "I know him as Shaman of the Mountain. He came to me when I lived in Taos, New Mexico, in the nineties and he channeled through me for about six years."

"Correct," she said, "and then he integrated within your consciousness, and you continue to carry his medicine and his wisdom."

I was surprised to hear that he continued to reside in my energy field. Yet, I often speak healing words or touch someone with my hands and I am surprised by the impact of my words and my hands! "Shaman of the Mountain, I welcome you back!" Imagine my surprise when I intuited a voice in my inner ear saying, *"I never left."*

December 7, 2016

I am grateful to be a student among seasoned prayers at Glad Helpers Prayer and Meditation group at A.R.E. in Virginia Beach. I am a quiet observer. Several of the members have prayed together for years. I am a newcomer and nobody has expectations of me.

That all changed when I sat in Elaine Singer's healing chair for laying on of hands healing. She whispered in my ear that it was time for me to extend and expand my healing gifts. She suggested that I surround myself with unconditional love so that I could be an instrument of healing for others. Then she whispered to me that I was a woman of beauty, grace, and healing. I took a deep breath and at that moment I knew she was right. No resistance— only a sense of "felt rightness."

Later she announced to the whole group, "Rosalie has a pocket in her shawl, and I saw how she enfolded her angel's wings in the pocket, and I want her to spread them over all of us." What an invitation to be authentic.

In January 2018 I facilitated the Glad Helpers group at the A.R.E. Edgar Cayce Center. We meet every Wednesday from 9:30-11:30 in the third floor meditation room to meditate and pray for healing for people who have requested prayer, all the nations of the world, as well as ourselves. We follow the tradition that Edgar Cayce established in 1931. Everyone in the group is a dedicated meditator.

As I meditated about our group, I realized that Joy was missing from our commitment to meditate, pray, and offer healing. At that moment, I understood that Future Pull was at work on me.

In preparation for leading the dedicated group of volunteers, I collected several prayers that were Joy based as well as some quotations from Edgar Cayce about Joy. I also said out loud that if books were written about the Joy of Cooking and the Joy of Sex, why not The Joy of Healing?

Being inclusive, I asked the healers in the group to ground themselves in Joy before calling out the names of people who had requested healing. People looked surprised. I had broken rank with my traditional role and the outline that we follow. People smiled. Before the hands-on healing part of our meeting, I invited everyone in the room to remember a Joyful event of the past week. A few looked like they needed a prompt and I suggested if they were not aware of such an event, to use their imaginations and create one. During the third week of facilitating the group, I giggled, as I understood that my role as a leader and my soul purpose were one.

I learned that I feel more connected to my soul when I listen and dare to trust that I will be received.

I appreciated how everyone was excited to add Joy to our healing ritual.

And I will continue to step into spiritual leadership when I know it is mine to do.

March 2018

During Glad Helpers, I felt a cascade of energy at the top of my head around my crown chakra. The sensation felt as if heavy raindrops were hitting the top of my head. The pressure accelerated and then it felt like hailstones bombarding my head. Somehow my crown chakra "unloosened." Usually sleep is integration time for me, but I boarded an airplane the same day to join my daughter in Puerto Rico for my four-day 74th birthday celebration and there was no time for sleep.

During most of our vacation, I felt energetic confusion that bordered on being overwhelmed. I did not understand that the energy that had been unloosened needed to be grounded in my physical body. I had also forgotten that the crown chakra is about pure Being.

When I returned home, I was sicker than I could ever remember. For the first three days I slept fitfully and realized I was writing in my mind or wrestling with the question: "What is reality?" At times I was far away from my body and more comfortable in that dimension because being in my body was physically painful. Instinctively, I challenged myself to remain in my body instead of going out of the body to ask for help.

Looking back, that was probably the only way my guides could ensure that I would not read, write, process, or even contemplate.

I felt as if I was going crazy with "just being." Yet Being and emptiness were my soul's agenda. Distracting myself by filling up with words, ideas, or even meditation and prayer felt wrong. Breathe and be. Repeat until I fell asleep. Then repeat when I awoke. Let all else go. Coming into the emptiness of pure Being—by "just being"—was hard work for me.

I understand that I must be fully embodied to be receptive and safe while bridging the spiritual realms. Unless I fully inhabit my physical body, I cannot be fully grounded in other dimensions of consciousness.

February 10, 2016
Healing cannot occur if we do not accept our worthiness even if doing so shakes up our view of the world and how we interact with others. Self-worthiness has to be integrated before manifestation and healing happens.

THE POWER OF INTENTIONAL PRAYER

Each day I create time to be in holy alignment because uplifting prayer keeps me out of my Personal Story. For me, prayer is a collaborative experience that connects me to the spaciousness of Being. When I lived out of Personal Story, most of my prayers were based on demanding and whining. Now I do my best to pray from a place of Joy—not lack. I approach prayer slowly, one step at a time until I create a sense of comfortability.

My memory is fluid. I remember tiptoeing into my Grandmother's living room many evenings after work and seeing her sitting at her wooden kitchen table with her head bowed and her hands clasped in front of her. I remember how her chin quivered as she moved her mouth in silent prayer. I remember how the tiny blue veins stood out in her folded hands. When she prayed, her apartment felt filled with holiness. I never interrupted her, and she never invited me to join her. Prayer, for her, was solitary.

My daily prayer is to live Spirit until my will is one with God's desire. Prayers that come from the depths of our hearts carry the deepest power. I have discovered that the more passionate my prayer, the more potential for upliftment and healing. At times I have experienced grace when Spirit comes through and prayers flow through me. I have adopted the mystic's way of Being: prolonged prayer to access depth.

Here are a few prayer lines that I discovered in my journals:

May I experience the deep love within me, and may my heart be open to receive the Divine.

May I surrender into your compassionate love,

Releasing all that I think I know,

Releasing all of who I think I am,

And being willing to be birthed again and again and again.

Help me to grow daily into the spaciousness of my heart.

I pray to go deeper and know this depth as home.

Help me to discern between firm, fierce, and gentle strength.

Help me to make my will one with God's desire.

I pray for forgiveness when forgiveness is necessary. Forgiving others and accepting forgiveness for myself.

I pray for a peaceful life and world and sustained creativity and Joy.

May all beings be blessed.

For this, I am grateful.

When I re-enter the world after praying, I do my best to return to my everyday life knowing that my eternal connection with the Creator has been completed so that I can rest in Truth. The next step is living my prayers in the world.

The effects of saying "Yes" to the frequency of Future Pull are not always immediate. Like any other apprenticeship, learning is accumulative. Almost two years elapsed between the March 2018 journal entry above and the following breakthrough event.

October 7, 2018
During the laying-on of hands healing prayer at Glad Helpers today, I witnessed myself calling in the energies of Almighty God, The Almighty Father. Never in this lifetime have I dared to invoke such power. The energy that flowed through my body and out through my hands was pure light and it is beyond anything that I have experienced. I am more familiar with the gentle, nurturing energy of Mother Mary.

I almost stopped myself from receiving because I
questioned if I were betraying the Divine Feminine by calling
in Almighty anything. Yet I felt compelled from every cell in
my body to invite the Almighty into my energy field and then
was empowered to say, "Give me all that you've got."

A few months passed before I was credentialed to offer
laying on of hands at Glad Helper's. Inwardly, I praised
Almighty Father and Mother Mary before placing my
hands on the back of the man sitting in my healing chair.
Immediately, I was filled with fuchsia energy and I knew I was
channeling Holy Spirit. I trusted that the man from Chicago
was ready for the flood of healing energy.

When he sat down, I whispered, "You are in good hands,"
and he was! He began to tremble and shake as soon as I
placed my hands on his back. I maintained my focus for
about ten minutes as his body continued to shake.

Our breathing was in sync and he was an amazing
receiver. I continued sending healing energy as he released an
unwanted entity that he had picked up in the hospital where
he visits people and sings them back to health.

His wife sat down in my chair next. She too was an
excellent receiver. Her grandmother, who resided in Spirit,
channeled healing energy through me with a message for her.
Later the woman told me that her grandmother's name was
Rose. When I told her my name, she said, "No, your name
is Angel." She thanked me many times for my work. When I
replied, "The pleasure was ours" and looked toward heaven, I
knew she understood.

With this wide, steady healing light pouring out of me,
I realize it is difficult for anyone to resist. Just now I almost
wrote "Me," and I know it is not a personal me, but rather a
sacred aspect of me who is awakening to my authentic self.

It happened. All of it happened. After the Glad Helpers Group, we all went to lunch as usual. I had no words and no appetite. After lunch, I escaped to the woods and sat in the saddle-like protuberance of my favorite live oak tree. Still no words. Only tears. Later I cried again and then I sang, but I still did not feel grounded. Drumming to the trees helped me to remember who I was. Still later I wrote in my journal: "I feel like I have been claimed by reverence."

Although I had no experience or even a concept of bliss, my spiritual DNA strand responded, and I trusted that my eternal self recognized the call. Then I imagined that I heard John O'Donohue, *Anam Cara*, across dimensions whispering, "All holiness is about learning to hear the voice of your soul."

Intellectually, I understood that moving from commitment to consecration allows Spirit to take me where Spirit desires. However, this is not a mental exercise where I accomplish something.

I also appreciated that humility and praise are essential parts of reverence. This surrendering and re-awakening process truly brings spirit and matter into one!

A couple of weeks later Robert Powers reminded me gently of my long habit of attracting unbalanced, narcissistic men and suggested this encounter with Almighty God might be an opportunity to experience a pure, healing masculine energy.

The next day another evolutionary buddy, Robert Demers, pointed out that the Almighty energy was not a stranger to me. He reminded me that Jesus had visited when I prayed for help sculpting Bridget and again when I volunteered for laying-on of hands at the Healing Light Church in Etna, Maine, and once again when I sculpted the angel of compassion.

I re-learned that flow has an irresistible frequency.

I re-discovered that time both shrinks and expands when I am following the sacred awareness strand.

I appreciated how grace and surrender coincided and I discovered harmony of the opposites.

I feel free and unlimited.

And I will serve as a Resource for the Source with humility and praise.

CREATIVITY RE-VISITED

Creativity, intuition, and healing are all different aspects of the co-creative process. In *Awaken*, I referred to creativity, intuition, and healing as the three sisters. I grew into expecting that when creativity was my intention, intuition and healing would ground my process. At its best, art is worship and I appreciate when God works, God creates.

For at least ten years I have yearned to cross-train between writing and sculpting. Then I crab-walked and disciplined myself to focus on one art form at a time and grieved about sacrificing my other passion. Privately, I fantasized about what might happen if I dedicated myself to explore and enjoy the interface between writing and sculpting simultaneously.

Today I slid my chair away from my desk and retired from writing when I had no more words. Then I did a few Tai Chi stretches before I left my writing room to visit my open-air sculpting studio. As both an artist and a writer, I surrender to silence to hollow myself out to become empty before I create. Then I felt available for the erotic energies of the life force.

Before picking up a file, I said a short prayer. When I opened my eyes and moved toward my sculpting table, the stones, files, and chisels awaited me. A spare journal and a couple of pens are ready for dictation if I get inspired. Just like when I am writing, I always have a blank sketchbook within reach.

I agree with Edgar Cayce who believed that psychic ability and creativity are the same because they shared the same nature and the same source. Last night I confided to a friend that I feel as if I am being true to two lovers and no longer sacrificing one for the other. Then I remembered how a stranger at a recent creativity conference commented, "Your sculptures are so erotic."

I know the erotic as sensual, receptive, and wild.

Maybe there is a fourth sister: dream. Take a look at a dream that I recorded in my journal.

September 14, 2016

I returned home from Ireland and discovered the commissioned and unfinished Bridget sculpture laying on her back on the ground. Squidge, my former pottery teacher and friend, suggested that we roll her over carefully. I hesitated because I was afraid that she would shatter. When we lifted her up, I was shocked that her hard alabaster back had turned into dark, moist clay.

Then Squidge surprised me by saying "No problem, Rosie. Together we can create angel wings from her back."

Since I believe that we are all that we dream, I claimed my angel wings over my fear.

July 2018

For weeks, the twenty-five pound black stone was the last object that I saw before surrendering to sleep and the first thing my eyes sought in the morning. The stone and I marinated together all night. Then a vivid dream instructed me to hammer, chisel, and file away the outside of the stone until I uncovered the slender, green healing strand. I woke up determined to begin hammering and chiseling the stone.

Since I never work with power tools, it took several weeks to remove about fifteen pounds of stone before I spotted the green healing strand. I was excited to finally unearth the elusive strand. Then I remembered that I had no instructions for the next steps.

Whenever I am uncertain, the quotation, "All creativity is based on quantum leaps and uncertainty," Jean Shinoda Bolen, *Goddesses in Every Woman*, darts through the center of my consciousness. Then I meditated and prayed to keep from disappearing into my Personal Story. Clarity came via my intuition. I embedded a large heart with the green strand going straight through the heart.

As I hammered, chiseled, and filed, I remembered the summer I worked with Squidge learning how to be a potter. I felt obsessed with making rattles. Looking back five years, my creativity consisted of making hundreds of rattles that I later gave away. Now I wonder if sculpting hearts is another way of claiming my name as well as my authentic self.

Momentum claimed me. Within a few weeks, I was nearly finished except for one more round of sanding and polishing. I played with sanding only the heart and leaving the rest of the stone unpolished with the chisel marks intact. I almost rejected that idea because it violated all the rules about sculpture that I had learned. Yet I liked the contrast between the shiny heart and the rough exterior. Somehow the stone felt like a reflection of my present life.

When Sandra Bell, a psychic medium from Scotland, saw the finished sculpture she asked, "Where did you study Scottish runes?"

"I've never heard of Scottish runes," I said.

"You've chiseled the runes for true love and destiny all over this stone," she said.

I laughed and told her I named the sculpture Spiritual Alchemy. And so it is! (See photograph on page 169.)

For me, beholding beauty brings as much Joy as creating beauty. When I went out to get the daily newspaper, the early morning sky was a delicate shade of pink and blue, like tissue paper furled together. Beauty pierced my heart. Then Joy erupted. I breathed in the radiance and felt connected to something wondrous and so much bigger than I.

Then I remembered a quotation attributed to Buddha,

"The only kind of beauty that does not fade and that does not cause suffering is a compassionate and liberated heart."

Spontaneously, I offered a bow to the world. My neighbor across the street shouted over and offered a bow to me. I felt as if I was in the midst of sacred magic. I twirled in Joy and then twirled again in celebration. Throughout the day I felt the Joy of beauty and twirling.

August 20, 2018

Picture me sculpting outside in my side yard surrounded by tall, ancient pine and birch trees. The sun is shining, and a gentle summer breeze is blowing the stone dust toward my garden. I chisel intently on a twenty-pound azure blue stone that is a belated wedding present for my daughter and new son-in-law.

I looked up from the heart-shaped stone as I heard laughter. A middle-aged man and woman walked directly to my sculpting table. The middle-aged woman came closer and complimented me on the heart-shaped blue stone. Then she asked me if she could buy it. Before I could explain that it was a wedding gift for my daughter, she said, "I love it. I will pay whatever you ask."

"Sorry, this one already has a home."

"Would you consider selling this one to me and making her another one?"

I shook my head from side to side and explained that I had infused the stone with love, patience, and happiness for my daughter and her husband. Then she asked if she could hold the light blue stone.

"Of course," I said, "it is soft for a stone."

I watched as she caressed the stone, but I was not tempted to change my mind.

"Okay, I get it, but can I commission a sculpture from you if I ever get married?"

Before I responded, the man who stood next to her retrieved a small box from his pants and presented her with a diamond engagement ring saying, "I have carried this ring box in my pants for three weeks. This is the right time and the right place. Will you marry me? If you agree to be my wife, I will buy you a sculpture from this woman as a wedding gift!"

The woman looked as stunned as I felt! I wondered if his proposal was for real or a scene being acted out in another dimension at another time.

She screamed, "Yes, yes, and yes."

Their Joy was contagious. I started to cry as he got up from his knee. My tears convinced me that we were in real-time. I suggested they return in a few days and talk to me about what ideas they had for a wedding gift sculpture. I did not tell them that I was a minister and if they returned with a marriage license, they could be married on the spot!

A few days later they returned with a sketch of a tree. I confessed that although I am a lover of trees, I had never imagined creating a tree from stone. As they left, I giggled about how Future Pull always invites me to go way beyond my limited ideas. Then I marveled at the cosmic choreography that grounds all.

What are the chances that I would be outside sculpting (See photograph of the sculpture on page 169) and this couple would choose to walk down the dirt path next to my cottage? Or that he would be on the brink of proposing to her and that I was working on a blue heart for a wedding gift for my daughter?

Synchronicity is an aspect of Soul Story. I feel Joy when I am aware and attentive to how seemingly random events connect me to the energies of Future Pull.

Another example of synchronicity happened when my friend, Dee, showed up at my sculpting bench today. The night before she had danced around the bonfire at the drumming circle. Her Joy was contagious.

I had handed my friend the Future Pull gourd rattle that a woman created for me after reading my book, *Soul Befriending*. She had painted designs on the rattle that depicted stories in the book. As Dee danced around the inside of the circle in Joy, she shook the brown gourd. The handle broke and separated from the rattle. Then the insides poured over the ground. I was surprised that I was not more invested in the rattle, and then I wondered what the Future Pull message was for my dancer friend.

I was not surprised when she appeared the following day. She said that she prayed for clarity during the night. When she woke up, she acknowledged that Future Pull was inviting her to invest in her creativity. And so it is!

EMBRACING THE DIVINE FEMININE

Living in Fullness is the calling of the Divine Feminine. That does not mean pushing to make something happen. Being receptive is another aspect of Being. The challenge for me is to admit, "I just don't know and I want to know." Then I wait in expectation for what arises. As I move from Being—not doing, I experience more calmness and hints of peace and Joy.

Being authentic is being radically present in my fullness. That means I may be Joyful, creative, compassionate, sad, pensive, celebratory, and present in the here and now.

Expect me to show up as direct and also expect to be surprised by what I might say. Self-expression is the link between mind, body, and soul, and I do not always know what channel I am attuned to until I have spoken out loud.

Honoring my inner Divine Feminine required me to break rank with over-doing, over-giving, over-thinking, and over-achieving. Shifting my core identity from doing to Being demanded awareness, vigilance, patience, love, compassion, practice, and humor.

The Divine Feminine asks us to feel and inhabit our bodies. Information comes through our bodies and is grounded in our hearts. Opening our vulnerable hearts to experience the holy in our own body is also a touchstone for the feminine way of Being.

The way of the Divine Feminine is inclusion—expansion through inclusion. She also asks us to integrate all parts of the self. The feminine ways of Being thrive in silence, receptivity, reflection, and community. A continuous, unfolding, evolutionary process grounds the feminine. Her ways are untamed, unpredictable, and uncertain.

May 16, 2010
I awoke with the word "devotion" in my consciousness and on my lips. I am aware of how devotion orders and disorders in my life.

I believe we are all mystics slowly awakening to who we are. I embrace mysticism as becoming one with that which I adore. A direct encounter with the Divine belongs to the sacred strand of awareness that I consider our seventh sense. I do my best to follow the advice of Jan Phillips, *How To Be a Mystic,* "Leave the newspaper folded, the answering machine off, and the door to your prayer place closed to the world till you have taken the call from the One Who Speaks in Silence."

The challenge is how to show up in a loving and useful way. As women, we often judge ourselves for our own suffering. Our task is to allow our pain to open up to the pain in the world. In opening to the holy, we embrace our fundamental blessedness.

I am deeply aware of how women have sourced power within a masculine power model for lifetimes. Until the last few decades, I have not heard the words "feminine" and "power" in the same sentence. Historically, the feminine model is the use of power in service to others. For me, feminine power is about interconnection, integration, and openness.

The following mantra expresses the essence of feminine power:

We do not arrive, we process.
We do not learn, we remember.
We do not become, we are.

During my lifetime a new definition of feminine is evolving: a collective unfolding of life within the core values of caring, loving, interconnecting, openness, and well-being. For years I have returned to Jean Baker Miller's *Toward A New Psychology of Women* definition of power: "Power is the capacity to implement." Feminine power is about transforming our lives from the inside out through voice and vision.

August 8, 2012

Last night I dreamed about Ma Durga and woke up with her name on my lips. Throughout the day her name seemed wired to my memory. Finally, I went online to find out more information. "Ma" is a Sanskrit word that refers to rebirth and regeneration. I was both surprised and not surprised when I read that she is a Hindu goddess known as the protective mother of all that is good and harmonious in the universe. Also, she is a symbol of power and strength. I downloaded a photo of her and lit a candle and placed her photo on my altar.

Later when I asked how Ma Durga protected me, I heard the words, "By the fire of persistence." Intuitively, I understood that she burns away the old to empower new growth, and then she protects new growth. Throughout the week, I wondered if I had been a devotee of Ma Durga in past lifetimes because she is here with me now, again protecting and awakening me to my Divine Feminine roots.

Three years later, I recorded this entry in my journal:

August 10, 2015

I was sitting in the meditation loft in my former apartment with Georgia and feeling as if I had never left Stetson, Maine, and that my life in Virginia Beach was a dream. Then within seconds, I felt as if sitting in the meditation loft was another dream. I laughed out loud and whispered to myself, "It's *all* a dream, Rosie."

Only the presence of Mother Mary remained the constant and outside of the dream. The moment I opened to her during meditation, my hands grew hot. Then I said to her, "We begin again."

From deep within my heart, I heard her respond, "We continue."

Mother Mary's response, "We continue," tumbled me back in time to our first encounter.

March 23, 1993

Each year since the death of my son, Mike, in 1977, I dreaded the month of March because it marked the anniversary of his death and my birthday. Fifteen years after his death, I considered myself a veteran of grief; however, my heart felt hijacked when I realized that he had been dead longer than he had been alive.

I decided to drive to Crestone, Colorado, with two of my soul buddies to offer prayers and do a ritual.

The small church was empty as I entered and I chose a seat in the front pew. My heart ached. My eyes were dry and itchy. I had an urge to pray but I had no clue what to pray for. The bright March sunlight filtered through the stained glass windows creating colorful designs on the floors and walls.

The only sound in the small church was the wringing of my hands. I felt helpless and that reminded me of the emergency room doctor who said on my arrival at the hospital, "There was nothing we could do. Your son was dead on arrival. If he had survived, he would have been a vegetable."

I did not know how to begin praying. All I was aware of was how much I missed Mike and grieved his death and the future that we did not share. Although I lived into the reality that we had a soul agreement to communicate between dimensions, that did not ease my pain in the moment. I missed him and who I was as his mother.

I was filled with memories and regrets. I sobbed as I said out loud that my love was not enough to keep him alive. I closed my eyes and sobbed. Even with my eyes shut, I sensed the bright light flooding the front of the church, and I opened my eyes half way and half expected to see Mike. Then I focused on the emerging and consolidating energy in front of me. I was curious and not scared. As I slowed my breathing down I began to distinguish a face that looked as though it were made of shimmering light. It pulsated and vibrated rapidly. I was mesmerized by the intensity of the eyes.

The next thing that I remembered was I had locked eyes with the eyes that were reflected in the shimmery light. Nothing else mattered. From some ancient place beyond my everyday understanding, I intuited that the face and emerging figure belonged to Mother Mary.

She held my gaze and transmitted pure love and compassion to me. As her intense yet tender energy surrounded me, my heart overflowed with love—not pain. As I merged deeper with her eyes, she energetically invited me to come closer. Instantly, I was inside of her eyes observing myself sitting in the front pew.

Like erasing chalk from a chalkboard, all distinction between Mary and me dissolved. I no longer knew if I was the one sending love and compassion to myself or if Mary was the channel, and it didn't matter. The only thing that mattered in the moment was the immediacy and the immensity of Her healing love.

My next memory was of myself sitting in the front pew and filling up with loving compassion. My body felt light—not burdened with grief. Gradually Mary disappeared and I felt hot and flushed. Tears flowed down my face as healing and joy encircled my heart. Somehow I managed to stand up and slowly walk to the front door. Then I noticed the name of the church—Mary's Church.

For weeks I had no words to describe how Mary over lighted me. Each time I remembered and returned to the experience of remembered radiance, my heart was filled with love and compassion for Mike and myself.

I learned that I am blessed.

I felt overwhelmed by the Mystery of Mary because I am not Catholic and Mary was not mentioned very much in the Protestant Church of my youth.

I re-discovered how to merge with a Divine energy.

I appreciated that Mary's visit was the first time that I believed it was possible to experience myself as a meeting place between heaven and earth.

And I will continue to be a Resource for the Holy Source.

♥ ♥ ♥

Dec 8, 2017

During the night, I was aware of being surrounded by a familiar, irresistible energy. Mother Mary was present. Her Beingness blessed every cell in my body. Tears flooded down my face and bathed my feet.

The Presence of the Divine Mother reminds me of who I am and my unique form of unconditional loving that I bring to this world. I enjoy looking through the eyes of the Divine Feminine and seeing the whole world as sacred.

Not only does Mother Mary comfort me, but she also reminds me that I am her child and whispers to me about my sacred self. I am comfortable praying to Mother Mary for help because, in my experience, she has one foot on the earth and one foot in heaven.

I do not remember if she asked anything of me. I do remember that I surrendered to the sacredness.

"How much do I allow Spirit to run through me?" I tripped over that question many times when harvesting my journals. I am becoming more comfortable saying, "Give me all that you've got, Spirit."

I questioned myself many times about my capacity to embody my inner Divine Feminine potential. For me, the Divine Feminine allows, waits, trusts, and is receptive to the arising of Future Pull.

The spontaneous prayer that erupted from my sacred heart was:

May I be open to receive your loving grace.

May I come to know the strength of your Holy Spirit.

May your Divine Presence spread far and wide.

As I welcomed Mary and her Radiance, I exclaimed, "I am at your service."

I do remember lifetimes when there was an abundance of time to ponder both depth and uncertainty, but our culture has little patience for the Mystery and not knowing. One of the enduring lessons of living from Soul Story is welcoming depth and learning how to be comfortable with uncertainty.

Part of moving from commitment to consecration is allowing Spirit to take me where Spirit desires.

I learned that reverence is my heartbeat.

I re-learned that Mother Mary is part of my spiritual lineage and she shows up to surprise and support me.

I appreciate that moving from commitment to consecration allows Spirit to take me where Spirit desires.

I regret times that I did not intentionally call on Mother Mary and Almighty God for support.

And now I will serve as a Joyful Resource for the Source.

September 29, 2018
I desire for my life to be an offering to others. That's the reason I live my life in Joy, voice my experiences, retire from joining the drama with family and friends, let go of struggling to understand with my limited mind, and invite inspiration and the energies of Future Pull.

The deeper I surrendered, the sweeter the energy. Lessons came faster and faster. My challenge was to dare to step into the larger picture of who I am as well as who I am becoming.

I intend to create a sense of spacious well-being, Joy, and lightness of being by opening and grounding in a sacred and expansive place. Part of the soul's story is the journey toward God. A channeler reminded me: "Your soul purpose is conscious communication with God all the time!"

Perhaps that explains why I have an unquenchable ongoing need for cosmic connection. The path home to God requires me to center myself in my unique and authentic life. In a recent dream I remembered that Essence shares a magnetic resonance with the Divine. I am already wired to the Divine. I imagine the connection is like how I feel when sounding and resounding with Om.

INTEGRATING GRACE AND SURRENDER

My small third dimensional personal self didn't know there was another dimension beyond expansiveness. Now I am beginning to know that grace is another face of Joy and how the energy of grace connects us to Future Self. Once I connected silence with grace within my soul, I committed myself to embrace one day of silence each week. The day began with sunrise and ended with sunset. Until one day grew into two days of silence.

September 14, 2017

If I believed there were no mistakes, surrender would be a snap—a done deal—like the time I encouraged a client who struggled for weeks about making the right decision to flip a coin.

A deeper surrender circles me. I respond by believing all will be created in its own time and in its own way. Then I intentionally open to guidance from angels and archangels.

I am on the brink of understanding that receiving is a big part of surrender! For many months I have focused on letting go, and I have not been present for receiving.

My clumsiness in receiving is connected to priding myself on fulfilling my own needs. When I surround myself with compassion rather than judgment, I am easier on myself. I appreciate that I set myself up when I expect myself to know how to receive gracefully when I was raised with a deprivation script.

Consciously cultivating grace is possible—similar to consciously nurturing Joy. The phrase, "growth through grace" that is written in the Friends Quaker Manual continues to speak to my heart like the phrase "Know Wonder." Both are our birthrights. I am not sure what came first: the opening of my grace channel or my apprenticeship to Future Pull. Such a logical question to a dimension that knows no sequence. It reminds me when my grandson, Noah, at age nine asked, "What came first, Grandmom, me remembering how the top of my head felt when you kissed it, or you deciding to kiss the top of my head?"

Before I crafted my response, he said, "Never mind, it's all the same field so it all happens at the same moment."

I am learning that unbounded devotion beckons unbounded grace. How amazing that grace and surrender coincided within my consciousness. For me, Grace is the Eternal Love of God reminding me that I am loved. Grace is not earned by our actions but bestowed as an aspect of God's divine forgiveness. It happens when I am in touch with my God center.

August 7, 2017

My need for silence, beauty, creative self-expression, and water feels enormous. I am aware that my interior life claims me more and more each day. I have zilch energy to visit with friends. I also have no impulse or need to share my inner life with others. If I were in a relationship, silence would surround me in sharp contrast to my past way of being present. A wise woman once whispered to me that our yearning is our path.

December 4, 2018

Recently, I feel like my personal experience is catching up with my cosmic memory. I do feel graced, and Divine energy connects me to my sacred heart. For me, grace comes in many forms and it can be fierce, unrelenting, and as sticky as flypaper, or as gentle and free as a dragonfly. In silence, I take responsibility for being the guardian of my frequency and set appropriate boundaries.

Practicing equanimity involves responding equally when grace is flowing and when it is interrupted. In other words, I am practicing not being attached—letting go of thinking I am doing something right when life is flowing and believing I am doing something wrong when life is not flowing. Witnessing without reacting allows me to step back, take a few breaths, and sometimes to step into Wisdom. No matter what happens, I remind myself to maintain my inner peace. Otherwise, what is the purpose of meditation?

January 4, 2019

I often think of myself as the Queen of Surrender, and yet I have not surrendered my life totally to the sacred. Daily I surrender my need to know, name, and understand. Lifetimes of conditioning dissolve. Devotion and discipline merge. Humility and praise merge. Letting go and receiving merge. Only the mystery remains.

Humility has stalked me for a few weeks. Although I understand that the physicality of humility is bowing down in wonder, awe, and gratitude,

I hesitate to offer deep bows. Perhaps it is my feminist perspective that causes me to equate humility with being a doormat.

I reached out to Meghan Don, *The New Divine Feminine,* and asked her to talk to me about her experience with humility. She explained in hushed tones that, for her, "humility is love in action." Humility without praise leaves me either feeling neurotic or puffed up. Learning how to balance humility and praise took time.

April 21, 2019

Reflecting lightness of being is Joyful. I am at last understanding at a deep level that when I am in alignment with my soul and acting from soul space, which is 4th dimension, I am reflecting God's magnificence. I am lit up with God's light. Spaciousness is God's reflection radiating through me. Embodying my Soul Story involves re-balancing my inner masculine and my inner feminine.

Many of us are missing the quantumness of whom we were when we were born and embodied the truth that we are God with skin on. Saint Teresa of Avila's words resonate in my heart, "Without God I am nothing. With God I am everything."

For me, God is a relationship. I imagine myself as a gardener planting seeds of awakening so I can come to know the strength of Spirit. My prayer is: "Let this be a time of nourishment, of the deep connection of sensuality and spirituality and empowerment of feminine spirituality."

SERVICE AND JOY

Asking the question: "What is mine to do?" is the easy part. Taking action by applying the guidance creates traction with my soul. Empathy feels like it resides in my breath. That might explain why I felt compelled to rescue homeless cats and dogs when I was growing up.

When I saw how our government was treating immigrants, I was horrified. I considered going to the border and protesting and friends talked me out of that idea. Yet I knew I was called to take action.

When Catholic Charities announced a program where local people met refugees who had papers to be in our country at the bus stop to protect their safety until a family member or sponsor picked them up, I signed up.

May 17, 2017

The opportunity of being among the first friendly faces that the refugees encountered opened my heart even more, especially since I witnessed how fast everything could go wrong. For starters, the bus was more than an hour late. Earlier I had stopped at Harris Teeter's and bought energy drinks, fruit, and some healthy energy bars for the mother and her baby.

Rather than wait at the Citgo station for another hour, we decided to visit the nearby garden shop. When we returned to the bus station ten minutes before the bus was re-scheduled to arrive, we discovered that the bus had already unloaded. I panicked. I did not see a woman with a baby anywhere. I held back my tears and my fear.

We were there to make sure this family was safe, and this was our first time. What if they had disappeared like two women before them and I was responsible? I shook my head and looked around more carefully. Then I spotted a woman and a small child huddled next to the corner of the building. Although we were not given a photo or a name, I knew. I motioned for Dan and Jo Ella to join me. We approached the mother and baby girl with smiles and "Hola."

She smiled back wearily and let us know through gestures and a few words that she spoke no English. Between the three of us, we understood that she wanted to borrow a cell phone to call her brother who had agreed to pick them up.

Fortunately, two interpreters arrived, and I concentrated hard to listen as if full concentration would magically allow me to decipher an unfamiliar language. At that moment I made an intention to learn how to speak Spanish. I treasure connection and I wanted to offer more than smiles and groceries. I wanted to hear the woman's story and apologize to her for how our country had treated her and her baby girl.

The interpreter told us that Maria was from San Salvador and had traveled on a bus for fifteen hours. She feared for their lives. Before that, she walked toward our country for six months with her baby girl, who was now seventeen months old. Her young daughter snuggled next to her and looked around shyly at us. I wanted to know so much more. I wanted to share with her that she was a heroine to me, but I lacked words. We waited with her and her child until her brother arrived.

When he arrived, her baby daughter looked confused, but she went to him when he held out his arms. This was their first meeting. Everyone cried except the baby.

I wanted to know where they were going and wondered what she would do until her court hearing. I was relieved when her brother pointed to a nearby trailer park that bordered the gas station. We were almost neighbors.

When I told her through the interpreter that she had inspired me to learn Spanish, she said, "Alegria." Later I learned that is the word for Joy. I followed through on my intention to learn Spanish and studied for an hour a day for the next twelve months. When an opportunity arose to teach refugee children English as a second language, I volunteered. My updated new definition of service: love overflowing with Joy.

I re-learned how deeply I treasure connection.

I re-discovered how important giving back is for me.

I felt overwhelmed by Maria's courage.

I appreciated being a volunteer and witnessing a family re-uniting.

And I will continue to assist people who have left their homelands to seek a better life for their families.

I am intrigued that I became a Quaker and took a sacred vow to be the best lover and protector of Mother Earth that I can be within the same week. I know that Quakers do not take vows, and I also respect that Quakers listen deeply and follow the still, inner voice of God.

By joining the Order of Sacred Earth as created and organized by Matthew Fox, *Sacred Earth,* I dedicated myself to both ecology and social justice. I experience the Earth as a blessing. I also believe we are here as a blessing to one another and the Earth Herself. Furthermore, I believe that it is our responsibility to return blessing for blessing.

Thomas Berry, *Earth Spirituality*, said: "We will not save what we do not love." It is also true that we will neither love nor save what we do not experience as sacred.

Making a vow to be the best lover and protector of the earth as I can be means I hold the earth as sacred. Dedicating myself to the survival of our planet in all its diversity, beauty, and magnificence means I am now an Earth activist. The aftertaste of my commitment to be a loving steward of the Earth is Joy.

At Friends Meeting, I spoke passionately about how our Women's Bridging Generations Group has transformed me from pain to possibilities, from quantum physics to Me Too, and from commiserating about why the politicians that we elected did not vote with a moral conscience to realizing that I am the one to create change through my own passion and actions. Then I tried to explain that I felt as if our group was weaving our intentions and that we were being woven simultaneously.

I owned that I have grown complacent during the last three decades. As I aged, the activist in me retired from public protesting, writing op-ed articles, and confronting my legislators. Also true, I no longer wanted to be part of dualism: us against them, pro versus anti, and I did not know how to hold both polarities and wait for the AND to arise from the chaos. Although I have decades of being an activist, I lack a precedent for living in this time of heightened division, elitism, fake news, and unbridled hatred.

I recognize, given the present political situation, that it is time for all light workers to be truly on our game so nobody and nothing will throw us off balance. For me, that means daring to step into the larger picture of who I am becoming and asking: "What is mine to give?"

Then my role as a citizen and a political and social activist begged for more attention. The time is ripe for individual initiative. I can no longer live on promises or count on elected officials to be my conscience. We each must do what is ours to do.

I know that I am not alone. We are living in a new world and perhaps the call is to be brave in this unfamiliar territory. "Dare" feels like it is my soul's password in this new now. Knowing that I am not in charge of what arises is a relief. I am, however, in charge of remaining present and receptive until I discover what action feels authentically connected to my evolving Soul Story.

The shift feels like letting go of believing that I am "in charge" to moving into an expanded consciousness of being "in service" as a midwife.

Being a sacred activist calls on me to act with all my heart and then let go of the results. I also will take whatever time is needed to be clear about what is mine to offer the world as well as what I want from the world.

COMMUNITY AND EVOLUTIONARY BUDDIES

I am more comfortable belonging to myself and no longer seeking validation from others. Along with retiring outdated beliefs, I am also letting go of friends when there is no longer a positive energetic alignment between us.

Community is different now that I have consecrated my life to my evolving Soul Story. Truth has a unique frequency that is irresistible to my soul. I yearn to be with other truth-tellers. I yearn to connect with others who are challenging themselves to live in their Soul Story. However, most people are still working through their family stuff. As I step into my truth, everything that does not resonate with that truth falls away, including friends.

It is challenging to become ourselves by ourselves. We need evolutionary buddies to flourish and thrive. The more I reside in my Soul Story, the more I desire an authentic community.

What I notice most is that I have fewer friends and deeper levels of connection and support. Discernment reigns as I appreciate friends who were there for me when I was not there for myself and let go of others who wish to be part of my parade now that I have moved out of both Personal and Edge Walking stories.

I ran across a new word yesterday and it applies to the conscious community: Parea (n) - a group of friends who gather together purely for the enjoyment of each other's company to share experiences in life, philosophies, values, and ideas and to celebrate the simple things in life.

I am learning that sometimes being too flexible is not in my highest good. Likewise, over-giving robs me of perspective and energy. Putting up with toxic behavior is the opposite of loving.

In the process of taking up residency in my Soul Story, I am moving beyond familiar family identification and embracing spiritual family. Yesterday, at a local restaurant, I held the door open for an older woman who supported herself with a cane. She looked directly in my eyes, smiled, and said, "Thank You," in a deeply heart-centered way and I felt Joy arising in my heart.

Caught up in her enthusiasm, I smiled back, bowed, and exclaimed, "Many blessings on your day." Then she reached out and hugged me tightly. More Joy bubbled up.

Later at lunch, my soul friend, Mariam Weidner asked, "How do you know that woman who hugged you?"

I replied, "I have never seen her before."

She smiled and said, "Well, you certainly seemed like old friends."

Without thinking I said, "That's the way of kindness and Joy and meeting soul family. The energy is contagious in a good way."

The frequency of Joy permeates everyone and everything in its vicinity. I recorded the event in my journal so that when I need extra Joy juice, I can return to this Joy infusion story.

Looking back, I was surprised to facilitate a spontaneous community grief ritual. At a friend's funeral, I was aware that his daughter was becoming more and more nervous as the time to celebrate the life of her father got closer.

I knew it did not matter how many tables we had or exactly where the flowers were placed or even whether we put the food on the tables before or after the service. Yet she wanted everything to be right so that her father would have been pleased with her. The observer in me knew that he was already pleased with her, no matter what!

A few minutes before the service, I overheard her saying to a friend that she was afraid that she would not remember what she wanted to say about her father. I imagined her as a little girl and knew instinctively that hugs would ground her. Jeanne Crawford and Mary Pelham White were nearby, and I grabbed their hands and invited them to encircle Bob's daughter.

Without saying a word, we enfolded her in a group hug in the kitchen. All that I heard was a big sigh and I am not sure who or how many of us generated the deep sound. Then several women her age spotted us in the kitchen and joined us silently. Everyone in the circle began to rock gently back and forth.

I wanted to break the silence and remind everyone, "This is how we used to do it. Remember how we held one another and grounded and centered one another before we moved out into the world to do our 'real work'? Now is the time to remember and to act from the center of a circle of women who are remembering and supporting one another into Being."

I did not speak because I did not want to break the mood. As I looked deeply into each woman's eyes before we broke the circle, I sensed a coming home to the circle, and I gave thanks that I have lived long enough to have the courage to call us together to support community remembering.

In 2018, I wrote this entry in my journal:

Wise women came with me when I went to divorce court and chose to name myself with a spiritual name that I committed to growing into.

Wise women came to participate in a ritual when I knew my time was over in Taos, New Mexico, and I wanted to leave before the sacred Blue Mountain spit me out.

Wise women came to celebrate my daughter's first wedding, each knowing there would be more weddings for her in the future.

Wise women came when I finally disentangled myself from a man who was determined to eat all of my light.

Wise women came to my early book signings when I was not sure if my words and stories mattered.

Wise women came with their dreams, pain, expectations, and whispers to my workshops.

Wise women came with me when I swam naked in the moonlight.

Wise women came to me when I sat with my oldest friend as she learned how to die.

Soul buddies relate to who we are becoming rather than who we were in the past. They challenge us to admit how we are the source of our own experience and celebrate with us as we break rank with inherited beliefs that have become part of our core identity and yet keep us from deepening into Soul Story.

Good friends may listen and provide comfort, but they may not be willing to confront and serve as a spiritual mirror for your further growth. However, count on an Evolutionary Buddy to probe for the underlying truth. One of my favorite evolutionary questions is: "What beliefs are in my way of living up to my full potential?"

Evolutionary buddies risk your anger and even potential abandonment to serve as spiritual mirrors because their purpose is to support your full flourishing. They challenge by asking:

What is true here?

What are you willing to take responsibility for?

What choices are you making that contribute to your present life challenge?

What is the deeper lesson here for you?

I can always count on Jan Phillips, *God Is At Eye Level*, to hold my feet to the fire. When I told the story about reclaiming my Preciousness during her class at IWWG, she confronted me outside of class saying, "I thought that you acknowledged your Preciousness twenty years ago when you first came to the International Women's Writing Guild. We all saw and knew your Preciousness. How could you have taught without being connected to your inner sense of Preciousness?" she challenged.

I did not have the words to explain to her that it didn't matter to me if other people projected Preciousness onto me. I was a stranger to my own Preciousness until recently. The best I could do at the moment was to say, "Okay, but I was outside then and now I am inside."

Then she reminded me "If you are hesitant to reveal, you lose."

Another example of an Evolutionary Buddy happened in a restaurant in Santa Fe, New Mexico. The first time that I met Shoshanna Love, we both knew we were spirit sisters. When I gave her an autographed copy of *Living Future Pull*, she immediately asked me why I did not put my photo on the back cover. I explained that I wanted to include the endorsements and there wasn't room. She responded that when she read a book, she enjoyed seeing a picture of the author.

Then she snapped my picture in the middle of a busy Santa Fe restaurant and emailed it to me saying, "Put this on the back of your next book."

I did.

She was not intimidated or jealous of my light and frequency, and I felt the same way about her brilliance and creativity. She commented on my light several times saying, "You are alive and empty and that is why you attract Future Pull."

A few months later, I enjoyed a play day with Betsy Sweet and Pat Bessey, two of my evolutionary buddies in my home state of Maine. Although we had been separated by many states for about a year, we resumed our conversation as if time did not exist. We smiled at our dietary compulsions and marveled at how food and drink rituals merge. Then we moved on to sharing the painful, unexplored places in our lives. All before lunch!

I shared about my six-month apprenticeship to Preciousness. Without feeling like I was taking up the whole space, I spoke honestly about how I had not wavered from my Preciousness even when I was bitten by a tick and was diagnosed with Lyme disease. The diagnosis was a test for me because in the past I responded to illness with self-judgment. Without the Lyme scare, I doubt that I would have appreciated that the Lyme challenge continues to feel to me like a final exam about Preciousness. I passed! One of the big lessons that I learned was that I couldn't be in Preciousness and in judgment at the same time.

Throughout the day I allowed myself to be deeply and unconditionally received in my Preciousness! And I received Betsy and Pat in their Preciousness, too. I shined brightly and reveled when they shined brightly. Even when we voiced the messy, unfinished places in our lives, Preciousness reigned. After I had described some of my life experiences with Preciousness and its connection to self-love, Pat said she sensed it was more than self-love. She named it "Wholeness." I giggled as if someone were tickling my toes because my upcoming three-day retreat was called "Embracing Your Wholeness."

I have a tendency to ground my Preciousness in my accomplishments and the balance in my savings account. In Virginia Beach, I learned to count on "just enough readings to pay the bills" until the unexpected expenses of cataract surgery, dental work, and car repairs drained my bank account. I have treaded water since then. I did not realize that "just enough" glued me to Personal Story.

My guides added another perspective:

Trust your readiness to abide in prosperity by trusting love.

Trust that Blessings abound even if they are not yet visible.

Prosperity is loving and blessing all you meet.

That adds up to abundance.

I know from experience that abundance and prosperity flow freely when I create room to receive the blessings. Trusting that I am capable of maintaining the flow is my next soul growth step.

I am precious. Period. I am Precious regardless of what I do, earn, or contribute. I am Precious.

As I honor my Preciousness, I also honor the Preciousness of others. One of my intentions today is to fall in love with as many people as I can because everyone is Precious!

CONSCIOUS PARTNERSHIP AND JOY

Relationships offer an opportunity to bring healthy closure to unresolved wounds. Yet partnership is slippery for me. Some days it feels as if the whole world is partnered except for me. Most of my single men friends are now with partners. Two of my previously single women friends now have special men in their lives.

I affirm my openness and yet nobody has parachuted into my life. I have a few men friends whom I enjoy, but a conscious partnership eludes me. I have treasured this quotation from my mentor, Virginia Satir, *Peoplemaking*, for years:

> "I want to love you without clutching.
> Appreciate you without judging.
> Join you without invading.
> Invite you without demanding.
> Leave you without guilt.
> Criticize you without blaming.
> And if I can have the same from you, then we can truly meet
> and enrich each other."

Few people know that I am open to applying her words into practice in partnership. I wish to co-create a conscious partnership where I am cherished and where I cherish my Beloved because I know I chose to be born in order to experience a soul-centered, committed partnership that grows and expands exponentially!

Yet experiencing Joy within a committed relationship felt as challenging as Republicans and Democrats cooperating to pass laws that benefit everyone. The bottom line for me is risking Joy in a relationship. Risking requires surrendering and I don't like to feel vulnerable.

I added this quotation from Carl Jung, *Memories, Dreams, and Reflections,* in my journal: "When it is time for souls to meet, there is nothing on earth that can prevent them from meeting—no matter where each may be located." He gave me hope.

Four years ago, while I was in John O'Donohue's home town of Connemara, Ireland, reading his book, *Echoes*, I questioned, "To whom do I belong?"

My answer: "To my soul and Future Pull."

I recognize that some of my yearning/longing to be in a conscious loving partnership is connected to belonging. It is complicated because I also know that I am not willing to abandon myself or my soul to belong. Resolving the tension between belonging and freedom continues to feel like a life lesson for me.

I question what drives us to a relationship. Men leave their buddies and their forms of competition and roughhousing together. At what cost? I wonder. How do men resource the gentleness and vulnerability needed for a relationship? What happens to the camaraderie they shared with their buddies after commitment to a partner? And for women, what do we gain by leaving friends who speak the same relational language of the heart to mate with someone who speaks an unknown language? What do we compromise and how do we grow? I wonder if both sexes had the necessary genitalia to create life, what pairings might look like?

At age 76, passion no longer has the driving power it had decades ago. Companionship and kindness have replaced passion, or that is what I imagine. Being comfortable within the silence is also attractive. I remember the moment when my now ex-husband said in exasperation, "Just what do you want in a relationship?" and I answered honestly, "Space and flowers." We both recognized the truth of my statement and soon after divorced.

Is all feedback projection? I turned to my community to ask my evolutionary buddies for feedback about a man who attracted me. One said that she felt protective of me. Another warned me about the difference between expectations and attitude and ordered me to be aware of my attitude. Someone else commented that the angels are watching out for me. Another was caught up in the romance of it. A faraway friend called me this morning with dire warnings. The last one who responded asked thoughtfully, "What do you want?"

The challenge for me is to dare to trust that Joy can thrive in a relationship. I have been celibate for 19 years. I smile as I remember that the original meaning of virgin is "she who belongs to herself." This marks the longest period in my life that I have consciously practiced being a virgin.

COLLABORATIVE EVOLUTION

More than ever before in my life, I agree with Jean Houston, *The Wizard of Us*, who said, "Now is the time when we must renew ourselves and live as if we and all of life is sacred." Then I surprised myself by writing: I didn't know there was another dimension beyond expansiveness. Now I know that it is spaciousness. Pure energy, pure awareness, bliss. And I know that spaciousness resonates with similar energy as our Future Self and entrains us and creates an irresistible connection to grow into authentic self.

Five minutes after I had written the above, I opened a book and spotted this quotation: A Tibetan master said the whole of spiritual practice could be summarized in two words: "Be Spacious." I agree because anything less does not touch hearts. Depth is in the revealing—opening deeper to the Mystery in order that all will come in Divine Right Order and Divine Right Time.

I am becoming more comfortable knowing that peace is my natural rhythm. Finding my own rhythm and allowing my natural rhythm to find me creates a feeling of magic throughout my body. Then I giggle because to me "Peace is Joy resting."

As a midwife of evolutionary consciousness, my place in the world remains in flux, AND I know what is real. Soul is real. Body is real. Movement into the unknown is real. Questioning is real. Chocolate is real. Love is real.

The words of Oriah Mountain Dreamer, *The Invitation*, inspire me:

What if you were sent here by something larger?
Not against your will or wishes
But in alignment with your deepest longing.
What if it was as simple as finding what you love
And letting it teach you how to live.

I thought I was finished writing after working with June Bro on her spiritual memoir. I was wrong. Future Pull had another agenda. Once again, synchronicity or cosmic choreography, as I know it, was its calling card.

Dr. Gladys McGarey and June Bro were friends and had other life-times together in Egypt. June was five months older than Gladys in this lifetime. Who would have imagined when I emailed Dr. McGarey to ask her endorsement of her 98-year-old friend's first book that I felt June's heart at work through my connection with Gladys. Elders inspire me. That's what happens with eternity friends!

Both Dr. Gladys and I intuited that we had worked together in past lives, and we were both intrigued to learn what the Future Pull thread asked of each of us in this lifetime. She remembered a lifetime that we had worked together way back in the years after Lemuria and before Atlantis. According to Gladys, we did not complete our project and we have come together again to complete the mission. I wonder what took us so long to meet since I am now a new 76 and she is a new 99!

We were both surprised that I was not "allowed" to channel information when we met together for the first time in December 2019. The guides informed me that my role is to hold the space for Dr. Gladys to remember because her intuition is connected to her sovereignty this lifetime. I agreed.

The only time that I had permission by the guides to channel during our five days together, the guides reminded us that we had worked together in pre-Atlantean times as "dream mappers." The job of dream mappers was to catch evolutionary dreams of the cosmos and broadcast the frequency to the community/civilization in order to align people with the future—one cell at a time. In other words, we received the dream frequency or the evolutionary imperative, translated the frequencies into energies that materialized, and served as a "coordinating" function.

Dr. Gladys knows intuitively that the verification of spiritual DNA is an essential part of her soul purpose. While we were together, she practiced becoming transparent to the transcendent. Since there are no veils when one claims the consciousness of being transparent to the transcendent, I predict she will complete her mission.

We worked together coordinating our energies and the emergent evolutionary energies that hold the information and legacy of spiritual DNA. This coordinating function in action feels like soul alchemy to me.

When I returned to Virginia Beach, I realized that Joy awakens spiritual DNA. Then the guides told me to remind Gladys of the research of Masaru Emoto, *The Secret Life of Water,* because our bodies are made up of 97% water. When I called her, she laughed and said, "Yes, of course, dear, he was a friend and we had many interesting discussions."

Love and Joy illuminate our core identity, our soul purpose, and our participation in a collaborative community when we claim our Soul Story.

My guides added their energetic imprint:

Evolutionary consciousness is the signature of the Eternal One.

Embrace your unique form of evolution.

Invite others to embrace their unique forms of evolutionary emergence.

Celebrate.

As a writer and an artist, I challenge myself to know when a piece has been completed. When I was a psychotherapist, I attended monthly supervision groups. Dr. Joe Melnick, my supervisor, challenged me frequently with the question: "Rosie, when do you know it is time to throw out the flowers?"

I wasn't sure how Gladys and I served as "dream mappers," although I do remember and record my dreams in my dream journal. Then I smile as I remember the first time Gladys and I met in Arizona. Within the first hour, we both shared a prophetic dream!

March 23, 2020
We are in the midst of a pandemic. As a light beamer and healer, I tune in daily and ask, "What is mine to do?" Tonight

I asked the question as I watched the slow burning embers in my fireplace. My answer came in the form of a Deja vu memory that spun me back twenty-four years.

The night before the fierce Arroyo Hondo fire, I had starred in my first book signing for *Healing Grief—A Mother's Story.* Friends joined me in Taos, New Mexico, for a celebration. Many followed me back to my casita in San Cristobal for an extended reunion.

The next morning, smoke filled the air. Everyone was ordered to evacuate the village of ninety people except "able bodied workers" who volunteered to dig a large ditch to prevent a backfire. Although I had no experience with ditch digging, I volunteered. After pitching dirt for about an hour, I heard someone call my name saying, "Rosalie Deer Heart, don't you know that during an emergency, everyone is called on to do what they do best?"

I looked up and spotted a flat bed truck with several Native American men sitting on the back.

"Come with us. You are not such a good digger, and you are a strong prayer."

Without a word, I handed my shovel to another volunteer and boarded the truck.

For eight days we prayed in shifts from the top of the mountain for the fierce wind to show its gentle face. Women brought water and food and then left to cook more meals and care for others at home.

After I remembered that experience in detail, I went to bed. Before sleep came, I asked for a dream of what is mine to do now, figuring that after twenty-four years, I might have developed other resources. The dream makers heard me and delivered the following dream:

I am walking down a dirt road toward my village in present time. Then I hear a loud male voice ordering me to "look behind you and run." I turn around and see a big bear that is about ten feet away and moving toward me. Instinctively, I know that running is not the way. The bear continues to come nearer. Somehow I overcome my fear and remember that love is the only hope of remaining alive. Instead of sending love to myself first, I offer the biggest bundle of love that I have ever felt to the bear that is now about two feet away from me. I keep my eyes open, returning the bear's gaze.

Before my eyes, the threatening bear shape shifts to a puppy. I am stunned and numb and in awe at the transformational power of focused love. I watch the puppy chasing its tail and reach down to pat him. He cuddles against my leg and barks. I scoop him up with complete trust and love.

Then I hear the man's voice ordering me to drop the puppy and return to my village. His advice does not feel right to me. Not yet, anyway. I needed to be sure that the transformational power of love would last. The last part of the dream that I remembered was walking with the puppy in the opposite direction of the village.

When I awoke from the dream, I understood the role of dream mappers. The sole purpose of a dream mapper is to introduce a finer frequency to community.

Love is the healing frequency. Love has always been the healing frequency. By affirming and femifesting the highest vibration of love that we are each capable of, we raise the frequency of the planet and re-awaken the energetic frequency of Joy.

Please join me as we affirm ourselves as femisfestors of Joy.

Thank You.

In Loving Joy,
Rosalie Deer Heart

SUGGESTIONS FOR THRIVING IN YOUR SOUL STORY
Harvested From My Journals

Practice unconditional thinking and unconditional loving.

Savor love.

Honor your Preciousness.

Welcome your intuition as your eternal best friend.

Embrace silence as oxygen for your soul.

Surround yourself with beauty.

Adopt soul buddies who invite you to shine bright.

Dare to embrace your Authentic Self.

Remember to track dreams.

Grow beyond what you imagine possible for yourself.

Expect and accept prosperity.

Affirm: I am a Resource for the Source. Use me. Use me.

Welcome grace.

Delight God.

Claim your sovereignty.

Acknowledge synchronicity when you spot it.

Discern what is yours to do and become a sacred activist.

Claim Joy as your birthright.

Engage in Joyful service for the greater good.

CLIFF NOTES TO SELF: SOUL STORY

My yearning is key to aligning with Joy.

Greater expansion and greater expression are the way of the soul.

Forgiveness and harmony occupy the same frequency.

A wisdom perspective is knowledge beyond dualities.

Aspire to love the world as God loves the world.

The ability to tolerate uncertainty opens hearts to new possibilities.

Creativity, passion, and divinity are interwoven.

A new understanding of service as being in my magnificence and overflowing with Joy.

Grace is our birthright.

REFLECTIVE QUESTIONS FOR SOUL STORY

What comforts and securities have you traded in for your freedom?

What illusions have you faced and surrendered in the past year?

When was your heart broken open?

What deep desire do you have for your life?

How do you support yourself to thrive and fully flourish?

When was the most recent time that you were aware
of receiving a lifeline from God?

What is your Presence in the world based on?

QUOTATIONS FOR SOUL STORY

"Even a wounded world is feeding us. Even a wounded world
holds us, giving us moments of wonder and Joy.
I choose Joy over despair. Not because I have my head in the sand,
but because Joy is what the heart gives me daily
and I must return the gift."
~Robin Wall Kimmerer

"Joy will become the music of eternity."
~Ruth Montgomery

"Everything depends on the intensity of your feeling,
attitude, and devotion."
~Muktananda

"You and the universe are lover and beloved."
~Gangaji

"Keep in mind always the present you are constructing.
It should be the future you want."
~Alice Walker

"The quality of your relationships with others
reflects the quality of your relationship to God."
~Edgar Cayce

"Joy does not simply happen to us.
We have to choose Joy and keep choosing it every day."
~Henri J.M. Nouwen

"Without God I am nothing. With God I am everything."
~Teresa of Avila

"Joy is the most infallible sign of the presence of God."
~TEILHARD DE CHARDIN

"The sacred duty of being an individual is to gradually learn
how to live, so as to awaken the eternal within oneself."
~JOHN O'DONOHUE

"I have a need to busy my heart with quietude."
~RUPERT BROOKE

"These things I have spoken to you,
that my Joy be in you and that your Joy be full."
~JOHN 15:11

"I do not understand the mystery of grace—only that it
meets us where we are and does not leave us where it finds us."
~ANNE LAMOTT

"A heart centered life is a desire for and a commitment to joy."
~JAN PHILLIPS

"Let joy be unconfined."
~LORD BYRON

"I slept and dreamed that life was JOY,
I awoke and saw that Joy was service,
I acted and behold, life was Joy."
~RABINDRANATH TAGORE

"It is God within us that loves God, so seek joy in God
and peace within; seek to rest in the good, the true,
and the beautiful."
~RICHARD ROHR

"The Joy that isn't shared, I've heard, dies young."
~ANNE SEXTON

"Be Joyous in thought and action and celebrate others. Since life is
your mirror it will reflect joyousness back to you."
~I CHING #58

NOTES TO SELF

Dr. June Bro and Dr. Gladys McGarey

Rosalie and Gladys

Rosalie and June

Rosalie's outdoor sculpting studio

*Wedding present sculpture for
Kelli Lynne and Josh*

Spiritual Alchemy sculpture

Addresses for Future Networking

Virginia Beach Friends Meeting
1537 Laskin Road
Virginia Beach, VA 23451
www.VBFriends.org
757-428-9515

International Women's Writing Guild
5 Penn Plaza
19th Floor PMB#19059
New York, New York 10001
www.iwwg.org
917-720-6959

Healing Light Spiritual Center
38 Stage Road
Route 2
Etna, ME 04434
www.healinglightetna.org
207-217-2697

Camp Etna Spiritualist Association
77 Stage Road
Etna, ME 04434
207-269-2094
info@CampEtna.com

Association for Research and Enlightenment
215 67th St.
Virginia Beach, Va.
23451
www.edgarcayce.org
800-333-4499

Glad Helpers
Association for Research and Enlightenment
1-800-333-4499 x7551
prayer@edgarcayce.org to leave a prayer request on voice mail